DESIGNING WITH NATURAL MATERIALS

Flowers • Leaves • Seeds
Nuts • Cones • Fruits • Shells

BEBE MILES

VNR VAN NOSTRAND REINHOLD COMPANY
NEW YORK CINCINNATI TORONTO LONDON MELBOURNE

First published in paperback in 1982
Copyright © 1975 by Van Nostrand Reinhold Company
Library of Congress Catalog Card Number 74-7780
ISBN 0-442-26574-3

Printed in the United States of America
Designed by Donald E. Munson
Drawings by Elsie Trefz
Photographs by the author

Van Nostrand Reinhold Company
135 West 50th Street,
New York, NY 10020

Van Nostrand Reinhold Ltd.
1410 Birchmount Road,
Scarborough, Ontario M1P 2E7

Van Nostrand Reinhold Australia Pty. Ltd.
17 Queen Street,
Mitcham, Victoria 3132

Van Nostrand Reinhold Company Ltd.
Molly Millars Lane, Wokingham,
Berkshire, England RG11 2PY

Cloth edition published 1975 by
Van Nostrand Reinhold Company

16 15 14 13 12 11 10 9 8 7 6 5 4 3 2 1

contents

Color plates on pages 65–68.

Fig. C-1. Large beech burrs were sprayed green for this tree.
Fig. C-2. Sprigs of Japanese holly decorate this live crab apple tree.
Fig. C-3. Tree plaque for Christmas is nearly 2 ft. tall.
Fig. C-4. Christmas swag made from juniper prunings.
Fig. C-5. The gumdrop tree is just for fun.
Fig. C-6. White pine foliage and cones adapt well to a round wicker frame.
Fig. C-7. Outdoor heritage wreath is at least 10 years old.
Fig. C-8. Turkeys, fruits, and nuts on a meat platter for the Thanksgiving table.
Fig. C-9. Kissing ball of live holly prunings and sphagnum moss.
Fig. C-10. Nut tree combines with greens and nuts for the holiday table.

Fig. C-11. A soft wreath of artemisia and rabbit-foot clover for springtime.
Fig. C-12. Silver King artemisia makes a bold wreath for autumn.
Fig. C-13. Red-dyed pearly everlasting decorates a Christmas artemisia wreath.
Fig. C-14. Gilded holly leaves make a bright accent for a wreath.
Fig. C-15. Magnolia leaves and pearly everlasting furnish a fall accent.
Fig. C-16. Red hot peppers and tansy to decorate the holiday kitchen.
Fig. C-17. Gold angels and ribbon turn a plain evening primrose wreath almost gaudy.
Fig. C-18. Dried hydrangea flowers make a wreath with quiet dignity.
Fig. C-19. Fancy ribbon dresses up a heritage wreath.
Fig. C-20. Dried flowers ready to live forever under glass.
Fig. C-21. Washington prepares to cross the Delaware in a boat made from an avocado shell and balsa wood.
Fig. C-22. Which one is the wise old owl?
Figs. C-23 and C-24. Two sides of a large dried arrangement for a brandy snifter.
Fig. C-25. What child can resist the magic of a Christmas box?
Fig. C-26. Citrus skin flowers decorate a plaque of birch bark.
Fig. C-27. Parent and owlet on a sycamore log.
Fig. C-28. An old frame gets a new kind of picture.

Fig. C-29. Candle ring can double as a wreath.
Fig. C-30. Candle ring made for springtime.
Fig. C-31. Hanging features trophies from the seashore.
Fig. C-32. A beautiful door deserves a worthy decoration. Flat green wreaths of juniper and cherry laurel set off identical heritage wreaths made for these double doors.
Fig. C-33. Bobeche of natural materials.
Fig. C-34. Candle ring ready for Halloween.
Fig. C-35. Squat Christmas candle suits a shorter ring.
Fig. C-36. Tall glass candle required a larger, higher candle ring.

introduction

Even the least dedicated naturalist must wonder at the infinite inventiveness of God. The variety in shape and form, in size and color, of the natural world boggles mortal imagination. Rather than growing jaded from experience, I find my awe increasing. Collecting raw materials for the projects described in this book hammers the message home.

Pine cones, for example, come in bewildering variety. One West Coast pine normally produces cones nearly 2 ft. long, while a hemlock on neighboring slopes bears miniatures of less than 1 in. Seed pods of other trees, shrubs, and plants take every possible form, and seashells are equally diverse.

You must, of course, take time to look, but your appreciation will increase if you have a purpose in looking. If you want to make decorations with natural materials, you will see your own property (and everyone else's too) with new eyes. Every garden and roadside contains a wealth of raw materials for those who are clever enough to recognize them.

I am sick of the sight and smell and feel of plastic. Its durability, once a desirable characteristic, has become a liability, for it cannot be disposed of without polluting the environment.

Much of the plastic greenery I see nowadays looks "sick" even in the strictest sense of the word. I suspect the plastic batches are not mixed properly; foliage often has an odd yellow or brown cast that in the garden would shriek for attention. Flowers can suffer from many strange diseases, which are manifested by odd color symptoms. The world has reached a nadir when one is offered for sale plastic flowers and leaves which look diseased or past their prime.

If the energy crisis reduces the amount of available plastic, we shall all be better off. Some very ugly decorations will never be made, and the petrochemicals thus conserved can be used where they will do more good. A peripheral benefit will be that all of us will take a closer look at what God has provided.

Some will be inspired to grow more species in their gardens. Such action will not only be beneficial to their health, mental as well as physical, but also to their environments and to the aesthetic pleasure of everyone around them. Others will reap a monetary profit, for there are always people who cannot or will not do anything for themselves. You don't have to be an accountant to see that if you sell something made from raw materials which cost next to nothing, you are likely to make money.

Many of the projects in this book were perfected by members of the Doylestown Nature Club. Originally we started making them for an annual fair to support our various service programs. Our success was so overwhelming that we initiated new projects to dispose of our profits. Knowing the talents of our members, we were not overly surprised by our accomplishments.

What did surprise us, however, was the pleasure and comradeship fostered within the club by these efforts. We can recommend them to any group. Since we number nearly 200 members, small workshops meet in homes to make various items. We have spent many hours together, gathering and processing raw materials. We have learned from each other how to use them as cleverly and as beautifully as possible. Many of us have also discovered how to grow new plants, and all of our gardens and homes are lovelier as a result.

There is a satisfaction in making one's own decorations that answers a hunger in the least creative of us. And there is a warmth in bestowing a gift of one's own manufacture that is hard to beat. If you are really artistically talented, these pages will be merely a starting point for your own imagination. But I certainly empathize with those who are not so sure of themselves, and I have described the projects thoroughly, adapting them for beginners in many cases. You will learn mechanical details to make your job easier. I hope that you will be inspired in the process to take a new look at the natural world around you and to decide that it is well worth preserving in all its beauty and variety.

Parts of several chapters were originally published in magazines. Grateful acknowledgment is made to *Flower and Garden* and to *Horticulture* for permission to use material previously printed in these magazines. Thanks must also be given to Diane, Vicky, and Robin, who have helped me immensely with last-minute details.

1
supplies, raw materials, and how to prepare them

Fig. 1-1. Cones from two different spruce trees show how sizes vary.

Fig. 1-2. Components of this hanging were collected at the seashore.

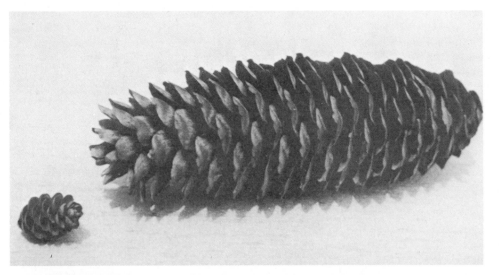

Long before supermarkets and neighborhood butchers existed, an astute cook began the recipe for rabbit stew with, "First, catch your hare." This practical advice is a good watchword for anyone who works with natural materials.

You probably will have to purchase at least a few items such as starflowers and other dried everlastings, which require hot climates, or odd cones from other parts of the world. But if you do much of this work (and it becomes more intriguing the deeper into it you go) the cost and trouble of buying all that you need becomes insupportable. Providing for yourself most of the cones, pods, and seeds that you use is not only economically sound, but also gives a personal touch to what you make that is very satisfying.

Many people do not appreciate the usefulness of pine cones and will be delighted for you to clean up their lawns. One of my favorite routes through Doylestown takes me past a Douglas fir, two horse-chestnuts, a rampant wisteria, and a group of sweet-gum trees. In season my pockets bulge with provender from one or another of these. Without permission I would not venture on the lawn of another, but what falls on the sidewalk I feel is free and merely lessens the work of the street cleaners. It is surprising

how much you can accumulate if you look carefully wherever you happen to walk.

Fall and winter are the best seasons for most pine cones, but many flower and shrub seed capsules mature during the summer and early fall and are best gathered then before they weather. Wind, sun, and water may change their color, which can provide interesting contrasts, but with time many of the capsules become too fragile to handle. You need to inspect the plants' development regularly. Many seed capsules, when gathered almost at the peak of maturity but while still green, retain some of their color indefinitely if dried under proper conditions. Left on the plant a while longer, the same pod may open as it dries, giving you a totally different shape and color.

Vacations offer superb opportunities for the collector. A very common acorn cluttering up the sidewalks of Massachusetts is totally different from anything I have at home in Pennsylvania, for instance. Enlist your friends and children in gathering. You may also make new friends through such efforts, and trading can be part of the fun.

Much of what I have learned about the art of using natural materials has been a mutual educational process among the women in my garden club. Formal work for our fair occupies only a few months of the year, but our collecting goes on constantly. Firm friendships have grown up among women who have covered themselves with pitch and glue, fought mold and migrating acorn worms, and suffered from poison ivy, chigger bites, and sunburn. What never fails to surprise us is how the interaction of agile hands and active imaginations comes up year after year with new variations on wreaths and trees decorated with all kinds of natural materials. We do know, however, that part of the secret of our success is our willingness to collect wherever we are, thus providing a great reservoir of raw materials for future inspiration.

Betty came back from California with boxes of chartreuse lichen and chamaecyparis pods, the like of which we had never dreamed of in our northern climate. Barbara's annual month in Maine means sand dollars and lovely bunches of sea-lavender. Anne's

trip to Williamsburg brought new ideas to ponder and enlarge upon, as did Jean's and Cathy's to Hawaii. Dottie returned from Florida with tropical pods for our store, and Virginia from Texas with a supply of cotton bolls and huge yucca pods from the desert. As a shell collector, Florence makes still another contribution.

The uncharitable might call us scavengers, but we prefer to consider ourselves clever aesthetic recyclers. Helen is the artist who suggests ways to make designs more effective, but many of our articles require no artistic ability whatever, especially once the techniques have been demonstrated.

I myself have no real experience with floral design or arranging, nor any artistic training or background, but with a little guidance I have become as proficient at most of our projects as anyone. I say this to assure you that you don't need great talent or ability to make the items described in this book. I have tried to make the instructions and illustrations as explicit as possible, but it is worth emphasizing that my examples are offered as prototypes only. Create your own designs out of whatever materials are handy.

Start collecting cones and pods immediately. The beginner never fails to be amazed by how many are used. The Styrofoam wreath in Fig. 1-3 is 12 in. in

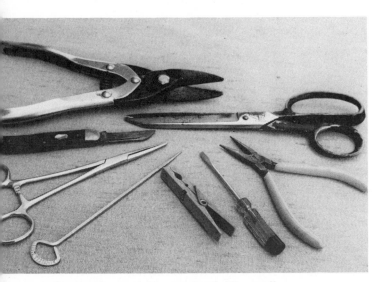

diameter, and it required 52 small spruce cones placed vertically to cover its outside edge. (Only half as many would be needed if they were arranged horizontally.) To cover the inside edge of this wreath takes at least 23 halves of large sweet-gum balls. And that's just for the preliminary trimming of the two edges.

At the end of this chapter there is a long list of useful raw materials with suggestions for picking and storing them. Two general rules are worth remembering in all your work: (1) never store anything until you are positive that it is bone dry; and (2) if you have any doubt about the possibility of insect life, bake the items in question in the oven at 150–175°F. for two hours. This last advice is absolutely necessary for any nuts gathered in the wild and advisable for cones that have been on the ground long enough to get wet. Nothing will dampen your enthusiasm faster than a room crawling with insects that have hatched overnight. If you have a large quantity of one item to bake, spread it out on cookie trays so the heat can penetrate. You may have to do the baking in two sessions, but it will be a good investment.

One further suggestion: some of the best flowers for this kind of work can be raised at home in your own garden, thus saving you considerable expense. Some need not be grown every year; one good har-

vest of quaking grass or strawflowers will last the ordinary craftsman several years. Many good sources are fine perennials which will add to your garden every year.

If you are planting new trees, think about the utility of their fruits as well as the beauty of their leaves, flowers, and forms. For a wet spot the sweet-gum tree is not only prettier than a willow, but in time it gives you a large crop of seed capsules. The cones of the Douglas fir or the Scotch pine are much more useful in craftwork than those of the Norway spruce. If everything else is equal, why not plant the tree that yields useful raw materials?

Tools

Some supplies are very specific for particular projects, but if you do much work with natural materials, certain accessories are worth knowing about. The essentials in my tool box include the following common objects:

  wire cutter
  shrub pruner
  heavy scissors
  needle-nosed pliers
  long, thin, pointed tweezers
  small screwdriver
  short tweezers
  two-bladed jackknife with awl
  metal skewer
  serrated steak knife
  snap clothespins
  round toothpicks

You can add a hand drill if you plan to put holes in lots of nuts, and a glass cutter if you want to make fancy vases from old glass jars. These are the only pieces of equipment that you aren't likely to have around the house or garage, except maybe the wire cutter. Do buy the latter, because scissors or a pruner will be quickly ruined by wire. The wire cutter is also ideal for cutting pine cones apart.

Other Supplies

Glue and the Dip Pot

One of the really great modern aids for handicrafters is white casein glue, which dries clear. Elmer's and

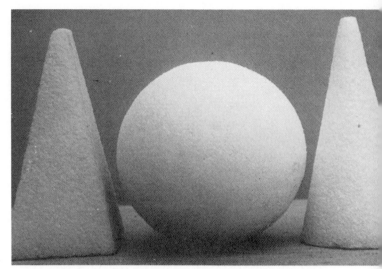

Sobo are two commercial varieties; they are much less expensive if you buy them by the pint or quart. A little dispenser bottle is also handy for some jobs, and you can refill it from the big jar.

Not only does this kind of glue dry practically invisible, but it retains its flexibility. Even after several years, it does not become brittle. It is also non-poisonous, noninflammable, and has no harmful fumes, all of which are important when doing extensive work at home. The only disadvantage of white glue is that it is not waterproof, but at least any spills can be washed away.

For many projects a dip pot for glue works better and takes less time than the dispenser. This is simply a flat-bottomed, shallow container at least 4 in. wide with an airtight top. Pour 1–2 in. of glue into the pot, then dip each item to be glued lightly; try to get enough glue to stick but not so much that it drips or runs. If you always replace the dip pot lid after you finish a session, the glue will remain in workable condition for a long time; add more fresh glue occasionally to keep the proper level. Keep a damp rag or paper towel nearby so that you can wipe your fingers clean.

Eventually the contents of the pot will get very tacky. This is what we call vintage glue. Even if it contains bits of debris, it is wonderful stuff for tricky jobs which otherwise demand propping or waiting for the glue to set. Save it for these jobs and start another dip pot for ordinary work. You can keep removing the hard skin from vintage glue almost indefinitely; the layer beneath just gets tackier.

Special white handicrafter's glues, which are advertised as instant, are horribly expensive, and they are no better than a tacky pot of vintage glue cured by time. You can make vintage glue in small batches by leaving a dip pot uncovered overnight, or you can put a daub of glue on two parts of something and let them dry for about an hour. When you press them together afterwards, the glue is just sticky enough to hold perfectly. With anything difficult, it pays to prop it for another hour or so to be sure of the hold.

Plastic Foam

Hopefully the shortage of petrochemicals will not adversely affect the supply of plastic foams, the best known of which is Styrofoam. It is the perfect base for many of the most interesting projects in this book. It is light in weight but strong enough to take considerable punishment, and I cannot think of anything satisfactory to take its place. So far, at least, you can buy it both in cast forms and in sheets and blocks. Ordinary stores may stock it only in the fall, but hobby and craft shops have a supply most of the time.

The green kind is slightly more expensive than the white and seems to be denser. In most cases the white is the better buy, since you should reinforce an article anyway if strength is important. It is more expensive to buy forms than to cut your own, but home-made cones and spheres are more bother than they're worth, and wastage is a big factor. Flat forms can be handmade by drawing them on the sheet and then cutting them out with either a serrated or a hot knife. Rings for wreaths are a toss-up; it's cheaper to cut your own from a sheet than to buy them ready-made, but there is wastage. You can keep this to a minimum by cutting concentric rings of decreasing diameter from a single disk. I save the trimmings in a bag for possible future use. Sheets from ½–1 in. thick are the most useful.

You probably realize that Styrofoam is inflammable and should never be exposed to high heat, but you may not know that it is also adversely affected by some paints. Latex-based paint has no ill effects, but spray paint and clear glaze melt Styrofoam away. However, these may be used if you cover the Styrofoam completely with floral tape or pods.

Oasis
This material is used more with cut flowers than for craft projects. It is really too soft for bases, but it is ideal for the dried arrangement. Since it is so soft, it allows easy access for dried stems, which are often very brittle. It is ideal too where you need moisture but do not want water to slosh around, as for hanging arrangements of live material or for articles that must be transported. Always soak it well before you begin so it is permeated with water before using as a moist medium, but have it absolutely dry for craft work. It is available in blocks, squares, and cylinders at most florist shops and often in variety stores or even supermarkets under different brand names.

Floral Clay
Usually colored green, this useful accessory is sold in every florist shop and in many other stores too. It lasts indefinitely but stays in better shape if kept tightly wrapped. Unless it gets very dirty, you can use it over and over. Work it in your hands a bit to soften if it becomes hard. For best results always make sure that the surface to which you apply it is clean and dry. I recommend it especially for securing candles.

Floral Tape
This is available at all florist, hobby, and craft shops. It is sold in rolls and comes in black, brown, light or dark green, and even with a surface that resembles a twig. Green is best for all-round use, but if the base is to be completely covered with other materials, it hardly matters. This differs from other types of tape in that it is flexible, so it can be used to stretch around things. It sticks to itself, but it can be unwound without tearing. The ½-in. size is the most useful.

Acrylic and Floral Sprays
Time after time in the projects to follow you will find the direction, "Spray with clear glaze." This acrylic lacquer helps strengthen many articles. It is also a good idea to spray fragile raw materials such as thistles or clematis seed heads to preserve them until you need them. Never do this, however, until you are sure the raw material is thoroughly dry.

Clear spray has another great advantage. It puts a sheen on cones, leaves, nuts, and everything else that accentuates their natural color. It can also be used safely on almost any cloth. A wreath coated well with clear spray does not collect as much dust, and it is easier to shake or blow off what does settle. Apply several light coats of glaze instead of a single heavy dose, which may not dry evenly.

My own feeling about colored floral sprays is to use them with restraint. If you have a bumper crop of dried flowers in one shade, it certainly makes sense to spray some of them another color, but go easy. Clear red is a hard color to find among dried items and well worth trying. Moss and evergreen twigs can be sprayed green for fillers, but the artificial colors are often harsh; choose the softer shades of green. Most projects are more charming if you stick to natural shades and nuances as much as possible. Too much paint can make a subtle decoration garish. Floral sprays do have a place, however, and I have often used them to brighten a faded article.

Always use spray glaze or paint in a well-ventilated spot, preferably outdoors. Take care also not to spray beyond the article you're aiming at; only the quickest rubdown can remove carelessly splattered paint. Don't spray on a windy day or when it is too cold, and always invert the sprayer afterwards to clear the nozzle, as the directions indicate.

Spray paint is far more expensive than paint in cans; use it only when a brush is impractical. Cans of gold and silver paint are handy. For small jobs I often roll a bit of cotton on a toothpick rather than using a brush, which must be cleaned. Small tubes of acrylic paint are another good investment; they dry quickly and can often be applied with a toothpick.

Hair spray can be substituted in a pinch for a quick strengthening of fragile items, but it is not recommended for any other use. Clear glaze and floral sprays are widely available at paint, craft, and variety stores under several trade names. There is a wide

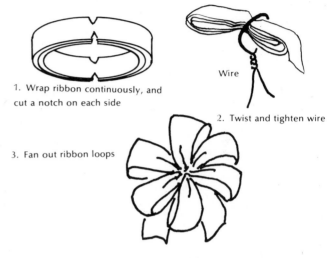

Drawing 1. Fancy bows the easy way. The secret is to wrap the ribbon continuously around on itself first. Wire can be substituted for the corsage pin.

WIDE RIBBON BOW

1. Wrap ribbon continuously, and cut a notch on each side

Wire

2. Twist and tighten wire

3. Fan out ribbon loops

range in cost, so shop around.

Wire

I seldom throw out a piece of wire. Even the smallest length may serve as a hanger. I have boxes of twists from bread packets and tags. But even the most provident must buy some wire. Craft and hobby shops carry a selection, and most florists have them in various gauges. The higher the number, the thinner the wire. The cheapest way to buy it is in spools, which can usually be obtained in gauges 20 to 30. I use the thinnest gauge possible for a given job, since it is easier to manipulate. For most jobs 24 is heavy enough, and for many you can even use 28. The wire comes in green, gold, and steel color, but not every color in every gauge. Chenille-covered wire stems are sometimes available, but you can do very well with less expensive pipe cleaners, and they are often sold in colors as well as white.

Cotton

This is another useful adjunct to your supply list. A little wisp of cotton in between often helps to glue two incompatible objects together, and you need large quantities to make wreaths of magnolia leaves. Cotton can also be rolled into balls to form bodies of birds and animals. For a few projects it may not matter, but those of us who work extensively never throw away the cotton packed with pills or in jewelry boxes. Instead of using expensive medical cotton we simply turn with carefree hearts to the bags in which we have saved these bonus supplies.

Corrugated Cardboard

Since it can be easily cut with an X-acto knife or any other sharp instrument, heavy corrugated cardboard is another supply to collect. It also costs nothing, while plywood continues to mount in price. For nearly all the craft projects in this book, heavy cardboard makes an adequate backing to add extra strength where it is needed. Rather than saving bulky boxes, cut the good ones apart at the corners. Flat pieces take very little room to store, so it makes sense to add this bit of recycling to your life.

NARROW RIBBON BOW

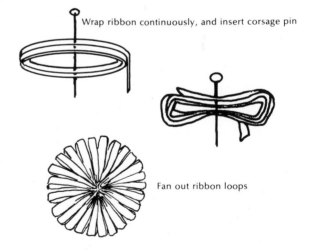

Wrap ribbon continuously, and insert corsage pin

Fan out ribbon loops

9

Fig. 1-6. Many-looped bows of multicolored, thin ribbon may be used to trim a large wreath.

Ribbons and Bows

I often spend more time on one ribbon than on several wreaths. For indoor use, however, the amount of time evens out. If you stuff the bows with tissue paper to keep their shape and store them dry and dust-free, many of them can be used over and over. You can also learn to make bows without a knot. Drawing 1 shows how this is done. Wind the ribbon back and forth on itself, and then either stick a corsage pin into the mid-point or wind wire tightly around that spot. With wide ribbon, clip in toward the center on both sides with scissors before wiring, then fan the loops out to make a lovely bow. (With wider ribbons, allow about 2 yds. of ribbon for a decent bow with several loops and fairly long streamers.) Always save extra pieces of ribbon, even when they are quite small; they can come in so handy.

Given the choice, I prefer simulated velvet ribbon for both narrow and wide bows. Grosgrain ribbon is stiff enough to make good bows, but it is more expensive. Satin ribbon is bright for indoor use, but never use it outside or under humid conditions, because it goes limp. You can spray it with clear acrylic, but this is at best a stopgap measure. Narrow ribbon is always a better buy by the spool, but the wider types are usually best bought by the yard unless you can use large quantities. Never tie a knot with the special wide, flocked ribbons, because the flocking rubs off. Wire them as previously described. Flocked ribbons often have a design in gold, especially on white, red, and green, and these can add a very luxurious touch to what might otherwise be a rather plain wreath.

I am not very fond of plastic ribbon. It doesn't make as pretty a bow, often splits, and is available in a very limited color selection. The narrow lacy ones, however, can sometimes be very decorative.

Velvet tubing and heavy yarn are also useful. They are particularly good for wrapping a wreath in a continuous encirclement or for a long tie to suspend a wreath. For small wreaths, you can obtain a dainty effect by buying the lace hem edging sold at notion counters. Give it a good coat of spray starch, iron, and allow to dry before making the bows. There is a good color selection at most sewing centers.

Never be afraid to experiment with two or more colors of ribbon in one bow; it can be very striking (see Fig. 1-6). Wide ribbon looks a bit silly on a small wreath or tree, but narrow ribbon can be used effectively on a large object. Just make lots of loops and several pairs of long streamers.

Florists carry special ribbon for outdoor use, which has a thin wire inset on either edge. It is expensive, but it often survives snow and rain well enough to be used another year. Don't try to tie it in knots; fold it over and hold together at the mid-point with wire. The metal insert ensures that the bow will retain its shape, no matter what the weather.

A steam iron is a useful reconditioner for old ribbon. Satin and velvet ribbons that are badly wrinkled can often be restored in this way. Old ribbon can also be used to make tight rosettes where the wrinkles will not show; with streamers of new ribbon, they look fine.

Still another kind of decoration can be fashioned from yarn. Wind the yarn at least two dozen times around the four fingers of one hand, slip off while holding it all together, and tie tightly with a piece of string in the center of the loops. With scissors, cut the outer ends of the loops, and you have a pompon which combines nicely with ribbon, thicker yarn, or a rope made of braided yarn.

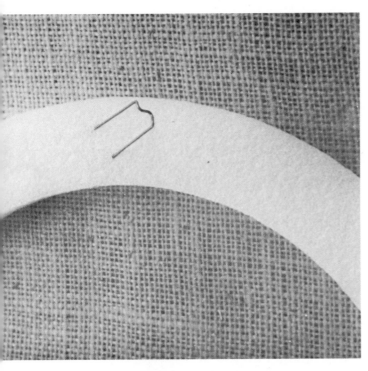

Fig. 1-7. Floral pin is useful for attaching greens or dried material to Styrofoam forms.

Figs. 1-8 a and b. Wired floral pick can be used with small cones and pods to make wreath decorations of many different types.

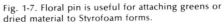

You can simulate a bow with cut, heavy foil paper, but somehow it loses character in the translation. There are spots, however, where the bow must be absolutely flat, and this is one way to do it.

Miscellaneous Accessories

Depending on what you're doing, there are other useful items sold in floral and craft shops. Corsage pins can come in handy for fastening bows to wreaths and kissing balls. Floral pins resemble straight hairpins and are used on some of the dried wreaths. Banker's pins are straight pins about 1½ in. long. They are good for using temporarily when gluing articles to a form. Floral picks are usually green, wooden sticks with a wire wound around one end. They enable you to make clusters of cones ahead of time for insertion in green wreaths. You can also use these in dried arrangements for items with very brittle stems; wire the stem to the top half of the wooden pick, and insert the pick into Oasis instead of the stem.

Cleaning Dried Craftwork

If you leave a wreath or any other project made of dried material on display very long, it will grow dusty or even develop cobwebs. Your vacuum cleaner is the best cure. Sometimes you can use the upholstery brush very gently at minimum strength, but other objects are too fragile for that. The safest method is to reverse the vacuum hose and fasten it to the exhaust. A good jet of air blown at the object will eliminate most of the dust.

Pine cones and pods are often dirty when you gather them. Many can be washed clean, but you have to spread them out to dry well afterwards. A sunny, airy porch is good, as is a screen near a heat source. Wash a few cones at a time with a scrub brush; don't just soak, because the cones fold up, and the dirt is trapped inside. Often a strong solution of chlorine bleach and hot water will brighten pods that have become dirty or mildewed. Let them soak about two hours, then dry in an airy, warm spot.

Storage

Before you put anything into permanent storage (which is quite different from the techniques of drying and preparation to follow), it must be thoroughly dry, otherwise it will mold. Green acorns, slices of osage orange, and immature pine cones are some of the worst offenders. Many of these natural materials will reabsorb moisture too, so it is wiser to store them in an attic than a cellar, although the extreme heat of an attic can dry them out a lot. My unheated garage has proved a fairly good place. Plastic bags are handy for storing everything, since you can see at a glance what you're looking for. Plants such as grasses and artemisia can be laid out flat in boxes or in bags hung from a rafter for future use. The latter precaution is advised if you have trouble with mice, chipmunks, raccoons, etc. Nuts, acorns, and seeds are best stored in glass jars, because mice will go to any lengths to get at them. The jars also allow you to see the contents easily. A few mothballs are a good idea for all materials; they discourage insects and rodents.

Because I store large quantities of raw materials, I keep two big, covered ash cans in my garage. Sturdy cones and pods are sorted and put in plastic bags after thorough drying, and all the bags are crammed into these containers to protect them from moisture and pests. More fragile things are stored in labeled boxes indoors, and a nearby mousetrap is baited from time to time.

Some method helps in the storing. Keep little things together in labeled sandwich bags, matchboxes, hard cigarette boxes, or writing-paper boxes with clear plastic lids. The idea is to avoid a search whenever you want a particular item.

Storage of the wreaths, trees, and other articles that you make is equally important. Crumpled tissue paper in the centers and between the wreaths will allow you to stack several of them flat in a big box. Always put the most fragile on top. Heavy plastic bags are handy for storing holiday decorations too. Put some mothballs in them also, and if you store many such products, label them on the outside of the package so you don't need to look through everything to find what you want.

The Recipes

My favorite cookbook makes it easier to put together a new dish by listing all the ingredients at the beginning of each recipe. I have followed the same format in this book so you can see what you need before starting a project. In all cases you may assume that you are likely to need the essential tools listed on page 6.

Filling in the Interstices

In making the many hundreds of wreaths, candle rings, cone trees, and what-have-yous that our workshop has turned out, one phrase has become automatic for newcomers: fill in the interstices. It is a lesson everyone must learn for himself. Until you have seen the difference between a candle ring that is almost finished and one that has had every chink and crevice filled in, you will not believe its importance. Large wreaths displayed in conjunction with greenery do not shout their lack of the finishing touches quite so blatantly as do smaller articles which are viewed close-up.

You may also wonder at the long lists of small seed pods in the following section and at the large quantity that is needed for even a single article. These very small raw materials are actually the key to really magnificent work for many of the projects in this book. Filling in the interstices becomes tedious, and often I put down an object after an hour of gluing and go on

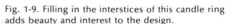
Fig. 1-9. Filling in the interstices of this candle ring adds beauty and interest to the design.

Fig. 1-10. Filling in the interstices of the same candle ring, side view.

to something else for a while. But I always come back and keep turning and turning and gluing and gluing, usually at the end with the help of my tweezers. And always I am glad that my patience did not give out, because it is those tiny things at the end that are the real secret of beautiful work.

The Raw Materials

Every year I discover new sources of raw materials for craftwork, so I am the first to admit that the following lists are not complete. Most of the things here are fairly easy to find, however; they are likely to form the bulk of your stores. What you can gather in variety enhances what you make and cuts costs. By all means, try anything you have in your particular part of the country. California and Florida residents will have many more tropical genera to add, for my experience is mainly with the flora of the temperate states.

Almost any substantial pod is useful. Very soft, fragile ones benefit from a spray of clear glaze as soon as they are dry. Keep a sharp lookout for interesting calyxes. A calyx is the outermost row of floral parts; it is often green during flowering, but it sometimes dries into a cuplike shape as the seeds develop and remains after the seeds are dispersed.

Some very long-lived perennials such as liatris, balloon-flower, or day-lilies do not seem to be adversely affected by seed production. Others may die out after a few years of heavy seeding. Almost all annuals and perennials have a shorter bloom period if seeds are allowed to form, so it is a good idea to let only a limited number of flowers go to seed; behead the rest of the plant to prolong its color and life in the garden. Most bulbs put so much of their nutrients into developing seed pods that they often do not bloom the following year; go easy on adding this extra strain to daffodils, tulips, and lilies, in particular.

This is not a botanical book, but to identify raw materials correctly, in some cases you will have to use botanical names. There is nothing to be afraid of. Many of them are already in common usage. (Phlox, magnolia, and forsythia are three good examples.) Some common names such as oak are so universally accepted that there can be little chance of confusion,

Fig. 1-11. Small spruce cone cut in half vertically provides a different kind of design.

Fig. 1-12. Top scales of a pine cone were clipped off to form a flower shape for later use.

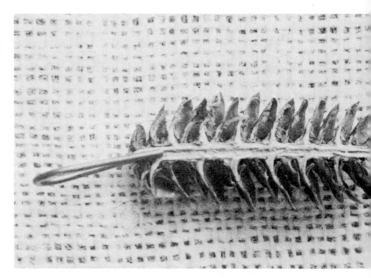

but popular names vary from place to place, and there is a real chance of ambiguity. Where there is a possibility of misunderstanding, I have included at least the botanical genus, such as holly (*Ilex*), to make sure you can identify the plants in question. Where a very specific plant is meant, you will find the full botanical name, as in butterfly-weed (*Asclepias tuberosa*), to make your task easier.

Drying

To prevent mold from forming, always spread out any pods, cones, etc. in an airy spot to dry well before storing. An old window screen set on some bricks makes a handy place for this; during the summer, put the screen on a covered porch if possible, where heat and air can aid the process but rain cannot penetrate. During the cold months, a spot near a furnace or heat outlet works just as well. Shake the screen from time to time, especially in humid weather. Items picked while still green are more likely to mold than those which have reached complete maturity, but they are worth the extra trouble, because the lighter tones add contrast to the more common darker hues.

Items gathered on long stems, such as artemisia or grasses, may be hung in bunches upside down in an airy spot away from bright light. I use the back of the garage, but an attic is also fine. If you want some curved stems, place a few of them upright in a container or lay them in small quantities over a log or any other round surface. Never use spray glaze to strengthen an item until it is completely dry.

Evergreen Trees

Gather cones as fresh as possible, even directly from the tree, because old cones often turn grayish. Unopened cones of all types are great, but they need slow curing to retain their color without molding. Soaking several hours in a strong solution of bleach and hot water will sometimes lighten the color of old cones; soaking overnight or on a screen in the rain often rejuvenates very old, brittle cones. Smaller sizes of all cones are always the most useful.

You can vary the effects of evergreen cones by cutting them. The smaller ones can be cut vertically with sharp pruning shears or heavy scissors, and they

Fig. 1-13. Immature cluster of arborvitae cones dries a soft yellow-brown. Those picked later will open to look like tiny flowers.

Fig. 1-14. Hemlock cones are graded by size for different uses.

make interesting cross-section designs. Long cones can be cut horizontally to form roses and disks; strong pruning shears or a handsaw will work on some, but an electric saw may be needed for very heavy, hard cones. Small pine cones can be made into various flower shapes by trimming some of the top scales with pruning shears. The properties of various evergreen foliages are discussed in Chapter 4. All cones are useful for something, but the following are especially recommended:

Arborvitae: cones are useful as tiny fillers; gather early and late for different colors and effects.

Casuarina (sometimes called she-oak): an Australian genus (not a pine, incidentally) that bears odd faceted cones; it is found in California and Florida and can also be purchased.

Cedar: *Cedrus atlantica* has a fine hard cone; *C. deodora* "roses" are worth spending money for; cones of incense cedar resemble flower pods.

Chamaecyparis: little open cones of hardy species are great fillers; gather while still green and closed and dry until they open. Larger types worth buying; often labeled as cypress cones in catalogs. Cones of so-called Atlantic white cedar, if gathered early in summer, may retain a purplish bloom.

Douglas fir: bracts makes these cones especially decorative; gather as early in the year as possible since old cones lose bracts; green cones often retain some color.

Eucalyptus: grows only in warm states, but bell-shaped pods are well worth buying for contrast.

Fir: Fraser fir cone has odd bracts; both it and balsam fir should be gathered early, since they disintegrate quickly when ripe.

Hemlock: you can never have too many of these beautiful little cones; gather as early in fall as possible; green, unopened cones picked from tree in summer and cured carefully are good for contrast.

Juniper: blue berries are long-lasting; foliage of many species will also last a long time if sprayed.

Larch: all species of this tree (not a true evergreen) are good. Cones often remain on the tree several seasons, but fresh ones gathered in early fall look like tiny roses. Small twigs with cones still firmly attached can often be found on the ground after storms.

Fig. 1-15. Even when almost closed, the burr of the European beech is far larger than that of the American species.

Fig. 1-16. Focal points for wreaths can come from anywhere. Left: dried calyx of a coconut. Right: dried slice of an osage orange.

Pine: Eastern white pine has a good, long cone; immature ones as useful as fully developed ones; gather both from tree or ground as early as possible in summer or fall. Austrian, Scotch, pitch, Virginia, Aleppo, piñon, ponderosa, red, jack, black, and lodgepole cones also worth gathering in quantity as fresh as possible. Jeffrey, digger, and sugar pine cones among the largest available. Table-mountain pine cones have an odd, bristled effect. When dry, all of these store well.

Redwood and Sequoia: closely allied species found only on the West Coast; hard, small cones very useful and worth buying.

Spruce: black, red, and white varieties have good, small cones; gather directly from tree if possible while still fresh. Blue spruce cone has an interesting, notched look. Norway spruce cones good for cutting into flowers.

Deciduous Trees

Both the fruits and the leaves of deciduous trees offer many possibilities for decorating. Generally, smaller leaves are more useful. New green ones can be obtained all summer from the growing tips of branches, and these also change color in the fall. The latter not only tend to be more proportional to your work, but they are also far less likely to be eaten by insects or torn by the wind. Especially interesting shapes and colors can be obtained from maples, tulip trees, oaks, tupelos, sweet-gums, sassafras, and birches. Press the leaves flat in a book between paper towels. Most broad-leaved evergreen shrubs, if picked while still green and treated the same way, will also dry a good color. Recommended: cherry laurel, variegated pieris and leucothoe, camellia, and Chinese and English holly. The following deciduous trees have fruits or leaves worth accumulating:

Beech (*Fagus*): small burrs of American and large ones of European varieties look almost like flowers; gather as soon as they fall in autumn so they are not dirty; nuts are great fillers.

Black walnut (*Juglans nigra*): gather round, ridged nuts in fall and leave outdoors all winter to get rid of husks. If you plan to use halves for owl faces, let them weather, and pry open when they split, or else gather

16

Fig. 1-17. No part of a paulownia tree pod is ever wasted. A group of halves can be glued together to make a large flower for a focal point. The star shape at the bottom is a dried calyx. The odd gray piece separates seeds inside the pod.

Fig. 1-18. Heritage wreath uses magnolia leaves, pearly everlasting, paulownia pods, and a pine-cone flower as a focal point.

from ground in spring; wash well, and dry in the sun. Pick out old pieces of nuts before using.

Butternut (*Juglans cinerea*): gather oval, ridged nuts in fall. Treat as for walnuts.

Chestnut (*Castanea*): use both large, prickly burrs and nuts, even when undeveloped; gather in fall as the burrs open.

Coconut: dried calyxes and undeveloped flowers make great focal pieces.

Date: cleaned seeds have a different shape.

Empress tree (*Paulownia*): every part of the seed capsule can be utilized; gather as they fall or from tree in winter or spring after they have dried.

Fig: small, undeveloped fruits dry hard.

Franklinia: fruits take two years to ripen and look like tiny, wooden roses; gather in spring.

Goldenrain tree (*Koelreuteria*): bladderlike pods, if gathered in late summer and kept in a warm, sunny window, sometimes dry reddish orange; otherwise they are yellowish tan.

Hickory (*Carya*): all species have interesting nuts, some a pale tan color good for contrast; gather in fall. Their shells can be useful too.

Honey locust (*Gleditsia*): long, curved, dark brown seed pods and big beans inside useful; gather as soon as they fall in autumn.

Hop hornbeam (*Ostrya virginiana*): odd seed heads resemble hops; gather before completely ripe in fall, dry on a screen, and spray with glaze to strengthen after completely dry.

Horse-chestnut (*Aesculus*): some species have spiny husks and shiny, large nuts; gather both as soon as they fall in late summer.

Kentucky coffee tree (*Gymnocladus*): both woody, thick pods and beans inside useful; gather and dry as they fall in autumn.

Magnolia: seed pods of all species interesting; pods range 1–4 in. in length. Gather from tree or ground in late summer as they open to let seeds out or earlier before the pods mature. Dry either harvest carefully to prevent mold. Dried seeds do not retain their original red color. Pods of *M. stellata* can be broken apart for interesting filler material. Use smaller leaves of evergreen *M. grandiflora* for wreaths; if picked green and dried on open trays, may retain that

Fig. 1-19. Two interesting tree seed pods. Left: silver-bell. Right: goldenrain tree.

Fig. 1-20. Sweet-gum balls come in many sizes. The old one on the right can be cut much more easily than the fresh one with a tail.

color; if picked from tree as they turn yellow, may turn any shade of brown; most specimens have rusty undersides. Store in boxes after completely dry. Old leaves on ground are more fragile than those gathered from tree.

Maple (*Acer*): gather a selection of various keys while still green; dry before storing.

Oak (*Quercus*): cups and acorns of all species among the most useful of all raw materials; they come in a wide range of sizes. Gather immature ones from ground or tree in summer; collect riper ones early in fall before squirrels eat them; dry carefully for a long time, or they will mold. Bake all acorns in shallow pans at 150–175° F. for two hours. Leaves of some species remain on tree most of winter and can be used as fillers in wreaths or arrangements.

Osage orange (*Maclura*): gather huge, green fruits in fall; whole ones can be utilized as bases for temporary arrangements of greenery. To make interesting flowers or mushroom tops for permanent wreaths or plaques, slice the fruits thinly across the grain with a strong, serrated carving knife; bake on cookie trays for many hours at 150°F. Then leave in open air to make sure they are dry; bake again if necessary. Always store with mothballs and silica gel, a drying agent.

Persimmon (*Diospyros*): calyxes of fruit gathered in late fall can be washed and dried to make flowers. Big seeds useful too.

Silk tree (*Albizia*): gather long, thin, green pods before fully mature in summer. If spread out to dry in a darkish corner, they will retain chartreuse color several seasons; ripe seed pods are tan. If you soak a bunch of fresh, green pods or ripe ones overnight to soften, you can bend them in half and wire together into a different kind of bow for dried projects. Pods of other leguminous trees, such as black locust, redbud, and yellow-wood, can be similarly used.

Silver-bell (*Halesia*): pick interesting three-ribbed pods just as they turn yellow in late summer, and dry in a warm window to get a brownish-orange color; if gathered later, they are brown.

Snowbell (*Styrax*): gather some round globes in midsummer and dry carefully on a screen for light tan accents; gather more in early fall as they ripen, since

both brown seeds and lighter husks are good fillers.

Sour-wood (*Oxydendrum*): sprays of seed capsules add interest to dried wreaths; gather in late summer and dry in small bunches, or add fresh ones to goldenrod wreaths.

Stewartia: calyxes and seed capsules both useful; gather as they fall during the summer so they don't get dirty. Ripe capsules often stay on tree part of winter.

Sweet-gum (*Liquidambar*): prickly balls extremely useful for all sorts of projects; gather as they fall in autumn and dry carefully on a screen. Immature ones often retain some green color, but be careful of mold since they take a long time to dry. Old balls raked up in spring cut in half more easily but may be quite dirty and need baking to eliminate bugs.

Sycamore (*Platanus*): balls very useful if gathered before they get so ripe that they fall apart. Gather immature ones as they fall in summer; treat nearly ripe ones with glaze spray after they have dried. Flakes of bark can be soaked overnight to flatten for use on plaques.

Tulip tree (*Liriodendron*): immature seed capsules found in summer can be dried carefully on a screen, then sprayed with glaze to strengthen.

Shrubs and Vines

Some of the common shrubs provide great material for filling in the interstices. In general, wait to pick until the seed vessel is well formed but before it has ripened to the point of disintegrating (usually in early fall). Those picked green should be dried completely before storing. The following are recommended:

Alder (*Alnus*): found in wet places; tiny cones are carried on twigs; gather in late fall and winter.

Bayberry (*Myrica*): gray, waxy berries very long-lasting; gather in late fall and winter. Make sure that you don't pick poison ivy, which also has gray berries!

Bitter-sweet (*Celastrus scandens*): pick small branches of the orange fruits just before frost and before they open to display their red berries. Strip off any remaining leaves and dry on a screen for future use or arrange in a vase immediately for a winter bouquet; they will open nicely on a few days.

After red berries dry well, spray with glaze to strengthen or use just the orange husks to make flowers.

Button-bush (*Cephalanthus*): gather when green or when larger, round seed heads begin to turn brown, and dry on a screen; may need spraying to strengthen.

Clematis: pick seed heads of large vines just as they begin to fluff but before they are completely out; spray heavily with glaze to strengthen. For small-flowered autumn clematis (especially *C. virginiana*), cut flowers off in bunches as soon as they fade and spread out to dry indoors. Most fluff out in a few days, when you should spray them heavily with glaze too; tiny white and cream balls are great fillers.

Deutzia: gather tiny, round globes while still green or later after browning but before real winter; great fillers.

Forsythia: gather small, pointed seed capsules just as they begin to open in summer, then dry on a screen.

Fothergilla: mature seed pods are similar to those of witch-hazel; whole stalks of immature ones gathered in summer even more interesting as fillers; dry on a screen for a few days.

Hazlenut or Filbert (*Corylus*): small, round nuts are great for contrast in wreaths; dried husks also useful if gathered before they disintegrate in fall; can also pick green and dry on a screen, but this takes a long time.

Holly (*Ilex*): dried leaves good for gilding.

Hydrangea: gather bunches of flowers in late summer and make into wreaths before they dry; can also be saved for fillers.

Hypericum: pick seed heads in early fall but before completely dry so ruff below seed head is still in place; spread out to dry; spray with glaze to strengthen afterwards.

Leucothoe: loose bunches of tiny globes can be used whole or as very small fillers; gather in late fall and winter; spray with glaze to strengthen when completely dry.

Lilac (*Syringa*): allow seed heads to form well and turn brown before gathering in early fall; great fillers.

Mock-orange (*Philadelphus*): small, round capsules look like tiny flowers and make great fillers; gather as they begin to open in late fall but before they get too dry.

Mountain laurel (*Kalmia*): gather bunches of seed heads after they begin to brown but while still sticky and spread to dry; tiny fillers.

Oleander (*Nerium oleander*): thin pods about 5 in. long split in half to look like outlines of flowers; gather as they turn dark; seeds are fluffy.

Pieris: tiny bunches of globular seed heads should be gathered in early fall before they get too dry; spread on a screen to dry, then spray with glaze to strengthen; great fillers.

Prickly-ash (*Zanthoxylum*): shiny, black seeds are great for eyes; gather in fall.

Pussy willows (*Salix caprea* and *S. discolor*): gather some in spring just as the catkins open; allow some to grow a bit longer but not to ripen fully. Cut branches and stand upright in a jar without water or break off individual catkins to dry; can be stored indefinitely.

Rhododendron: beautiful, little brown flowers if gathered in early winter after ripening but before disintegrating.

Rose-of-Sharon or Althea (*Hibiscus*): leave capsules on bush in fall until they open, then pick and spread to dry if necessary. Single-flowered ones best; shake seeds out for neater work, but keep some for miniature owl eyes.

Sweet pepperbush (*Clethra*): sprigs of tiny globes are handy fillers for dried arrangements; gather anytime in early winter.

Trumpet vine or creeper (*Campsis radicans*): dried calyxes and pods very interesting small fillers; gather in late summer or fall, spread to dry if necessary.

Viburnum: bud clusters of some species, if picked early before they open, can be dried carefully for a different kind of filler. Recommended: *V. carcephalum*, *V. burkwoodi*, *V. carlesi*, *V. fragrans*, and *V. rhytidophallum*.

Weigela: capsules make small, brownish flowers; gather early in fall before they disintegrate; spray with glaze to strengthen.

Wisteria: most species have fat, velvety pods. If picked in summer when almost ripe but still green, they dry a soft olive; later picking yields a velvety grey color. Shorter pods more useful than longer ones, except in large dried arrangements. Big seeds make good fillers; drop ripe pods on the floor to break open or wait for them to pop naturally.

Witch-hazel (*Hamamelis*): gather seed capsules of last year's flowers when this year's are in bloom (spring or fall); branches of fall blossoms brought indoors will release their current crop of seeds with a snap to entertain your guests.

Fruits and Vegetables

The following are easily obtained from garden or grocery:

Artichoke: small sizes most useful. If picked when ready to eat or bought at a grocery, cut in half, dry in a warm, sunny window, turning daily to prevent mold formation; after several weeks (depending on weather), will turn orange brown. Or stuff small

Fig. 1-22. Half a dried artichoke ready to be worked into the design on a large wreath.

Fig. 1-23. Halves of avocado pits were carved into these flower forms.

pieces of tissue paper between all the leaves of a whole, ripe, green artichoke, and put in a warm, dry place to cure as quickly as possible. Both halves and whole artichoke roses make excellent focal points for a large wreath or arrangement. You can also leave them on the plant to go to seed, but pick before they are quite ready to fluff, dry completely, and spray with clear glaze to hold soft centers in place. Cardoon gives similar effects.

Avocado: pits are soft enough to carve into almost anything from beads to flowers, but dry well on a screen in a warm place after carving. They turn a soft orange color with a silver bloom and shrink as they dry; thin slices curl and make good petals. Use halves rather than whole pits if they show signs of splitting. Shells can be cut into leaflike pieces, since they dry a dull green; whole shells also useful, but scrub clean carefully before drying on a screen or window sill.

Beans: all types useful for seed pictures; shells of ripe soybeans and limas particularly good if dried on a screen or left on the bush.

Citrus peels: excellent sources of color for dried arrangements, plaques, etc. Remove every trace of pulp and membrane, scrape most of white lining off skin, then wash well. While skins are still soft, make flat flowers (see Drawing 2) by tracing a cardboard template on them and cutting out with scissors; to make three-dimensional flowers, cut petals almost to the center of an entire half or scallop the outer edge, and fold into cuplike shapes with the colored side of the skin inside; stuff hollow with wax paper, and put rubber band loosely around outside to hold shape; dry on a screen in a warm place or bake very slowly in the oven. Spray with insecticide before storing.

Corn tassels: after ears begin to grow, cut off top tassels from plants and hang upside down in small bunches or stand upright in jars in a dry, airy, warm spot. They make creamy spikes for dried arrangements.

Cotton: dried calyx left after harvesting makes a large, starlike focal point for all kinds of dried work.

Hops: gather seed capsules while still green, and dry individually on a screen or hang whole vines up in an airy spot; spray with glaze to strengthen after completely dry.

Drawing 2. To give depth to a citrus peel flower, turn it so that the colored side is inside, stuff with wax paper, and tie or slip a rubber band loosely around the outside to keep it cup-shaped while drying; this flower uses the peel of half a fruit. Flat flowers will curl slightly by themselves as they dry for still another effect.

Fig. 1-24. A whole artichoke, carefully dried, makes a fine focal point.

Fig. 1-25. Peels of citrus fruits were cut and dried to form most of the flowers on this plaque. Various pits, pods, and seeds add interest.

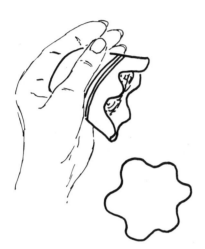

Fig. 1-26. Spent cotton boll leaves these striking stars behind.

Nuts: almost all eating nuts are beautiful for decorating. Watch for special sales of old nuts in spring. Empty halves of peanuts, English walnuts, and almonds can be used without wastage. Store in glass jars.

Pits: cherry, peach, and plum pits are great free raw materials. Scrub off any bits of pulp, or boil a short time if you have a large quantity, and spread on a screen to dry completely. If discolored, soak in hot water and chlorine bleach for an hour before spreading to dry. Store in glass jars.

Seeds: melon, pumpkin, squash, apple, and citrus seeds especially useful. Wash well, spread to dry on a screen, and store in glass jars.

From the Flower Garden

Some of the most decorative pods and drieds come from the flower garden, many from hardy perennials that provide outdoor color without much effort after the initial planting. Several of the most useful, such as baptisia, butterfly-weed, balloon-flower, gas-plant, and statice, make bigger clumps each year and are likely to outlive the gardener. The following list, while far from complete, contains some of the best varieties. The part of the flower that you use determines when you should gather your supply, so I have divided the list according to this criterion. It is worth repeating that you must keep a sharp eye on them until you learn their characteristics, so that you can harvest them at the prime time. Fall is far too late for many of them. If you are gathering each in its season, your work is spread over a long period and is not really burdensome. (Pressing or drying whole flowers in silica gel or special powders is a completely different process. The flowers listed here pretty much dry by themselves in the air.)

Primarily for the Flowers

Baby's-breath (perennial *Gypsophila*): great filler in dried bouquets; gather branches just as they reach their peak bloom and dry upright in a glass jar or hang upside down in a dry, airy spot away from direct light. Double forms are most useful. This plant likes full sun and lime; it grows eventually as high as 4 ft. and covers several square feet, so place accordingly in garden.

Celosia: cockscomb varieties are easy to dry; pick just as they begin to show good color but before completely ripe, lay loosely on a screen or upright in a jar in a dry, airy, darkish, hot spot. Plumed types are very graceful but harder to dry; pick when nicely out but before they show any sign of going to seed, and hang upside down in bunches in a dry, hot, dark spot; stems placed upright under same conditions will arch.

Composites: the heads of many of the daisy flowers like anthemis, shasta daisies, heliopsis, black-eyed-susans, and rudbeckias can be utilized. Allow them to ripen on the plant and gather when dry for brownish shades; for brighter colors, cut just when fully open, remove outer petals, and dry heads on screens. Gaillardias thus treated retain the yellow or red color of the centers very well.

Chives: pick just as the flowers open, and hang upside down or lay on a screen to dry; many other onions (*Alliums*) can be treated similarly and will retain some color. The heads can also be left on the plant until seeds form, then picked to finish drying for a light tan flower.

Heather (*Calluna* and *Erica*): whatever season they bloom, gather sprigs or long wands of these fine decoratives as soon as the flowers begin to open; hang upside down in a dry, airy spot to cure or place in jars for arching effects. Spray with glaze after completely dry. While fragile, they are wonderful for dried arrangements and can sometimes even be gently worked into wreaths.

Milkweed: both the pink flowers of ordinary field milkweed and the orange heads of butterfly-weed (*Asclepias tuberosa*), picked just as the heads open and hung upside down in a dry, darkish spot, will retain much of their color.

Pearly everlasting: if you gather this in the wild, sow some of the very fine seeds in a dry, sunny spot, for you can never have too much of it. You will usually find annuals or biennials of the genus *Gnaphalium*, and you can continue to sow some seeds each year to keep the supply coming. An even better choice is the native perennial *Anaphalis margaritacea* or the Japanese *A. yedoensis*. The clusters of tiny daisies characteristic of both genera can be used in dried bouquets, wreaths, and incidental decorations of

Fig. 1-27. Tiny dried flower heads of chives contrast with the huge dried seed head of related *Allium karataviense*, a fine spring-flowering bulb for the forefront of the garden.

Fig. 1-28. Pearly everlasting forms the edge for this bobeche.

every sort. Gather half your stock just as the heads form in late summer but before they open completely, and hang in bunches upside down in a dry, airy spot away from direct light; these will dry a soft white color and stay in tight clusters. Gather the rest of the crop as the season progresses but before the winter sets in, and hang similarly until dry; these will provide creamy tan, open daisies. They can also be dyed with floral spray for additional color. They do last just about forever, unless they get too dusty.

Pussy-toes (*Antennaria*): often planted as a ground cover on dry banks but may also be found in the wild. Gather in spring before the flowers are completely open, and hang upside down in small bunches in a dry, airy spot. Watch out for mold, since weather is not yet hot.

Roses: gather small double roses (floribundas particularly) just as they are opening but before they are more than half-open. Lay only the flower heads on a screen in a dry, warm spot. If weather is right, they dry into tiny, brownish rosebuds; this works especially well with yellow roses.

Sempervivums: hen-and-chickens and others of this tribe sometimes put out starry flowers; pick when completely open, and dry on a screen.

Statice: while annual forms can be grown in many colors, they are not nearly so useful as the perennial statice, which is botanically *Limonium*. It provides graceful, airy sprays of tiny, lavender or white stars. Flowering begins the second year after seed is sown. Germination is apt to be poor, but the plants get larger with age and last many years, so even one is worthwhile. It is very decorative in sunny rock gardens. Gather the stems as soon as all the flowers are open so they don't dry and blow away. Finish drying upright in jars in an airy spot out of direct sun, then store for years in a plastic bag. No one can have too much of this perennial. (When I refer to statice, I mean the perennial variety; it is often sold as German statice.)

Strawflowers (*Helichrysum*, *Gomphrena*, *Acroclinium*, *Xerantheum*, and *Rhodanthe* are some of the best to try): not always easy to grow but a good investment in time and effort if you plan much work

Fig. 1-29. Philadelphia's championship Flyers practice on ice made from an old compact mirror. The owl's tree is a dried branch of budded magnolia; the base is a cross-section of a large tree branch.

Fig. 1-30. Two sizes of decorative pods from the garden: yucca dwarfs delicate columbine.

with dried flowers. Sow seeds after the soil warms up and frost is over. Gather flowers of all types before they are completely open; if in doubt, pick buds rather than open flowers, because they continue to mature after cutting; if cut too late, they look ugly. If you plan to glue some of them on plaques or whatever, merely cut the heads without stems, and arrange loosely on a screen in a dry, warm, airy spot out of direct light. If you want stemmed strawflowers, buy some gauge 24 green wire before the crop is ready, and cut it into different lengths. Cut flowers early without stems, insert a straight piece of wire directly into the calyx below the actual flower, and push through the center of the blossom until it extends a bit above it. With needle-nosed pliers, make a small hook at the top of the wire, then draw it back down carefully just into the heart of the blossom where it cannot be seen. Put a drop of white glue on the hook before you pull it down if you wish, but usually the flowers dry tightly around the wire. Hang the wired flowers in small bunches upside down in a dry, airy, darkish spot, or place them standing upright loosely in a jar in the same kind of place. The latter treatment usually makes the flower heads tilt a little on the wire rather than sitting straight, which tends to give a prettier effect. You can always bend the wire stem later, however, to compensate for the drying. When completely dry, flowers may be stored indefinitely in boxes, but put some mothballs in with them. If you remove the flower heads faithfully, your strawflowers will keep blooming all season.

Tansy (*Tanacetum vulgare*): pick the yellow flowers only after they are fully developed, and hang upside down in bunches in a dry, airy spot out of direct sun; a good yellow accent.

Thistle (*Echinops*, *Erygium*, and *Cirsium*): various perennials are sold as globe thistles, sea holly, or simply thistles. You can pick off the decorative heads just as color shows and dry on screens or wait a bit longer, pick with the stems, and hang upside down in bunches in a dry, airy spot out of direct light. They may need spray glaze to strengthen.

Thrift (*Armeria*): both white and pink varieties of this fine rock-garden perennial make good dried heads for contrast in wreaths. Pick just as the flowers show color, and hang upside down to dry or snip off the heads and dry on a screen. Spray with clear glaze afterwards.

Yarrow (*Achillea*): pink and yellow garden varieties are good perennials for dry, sunny spots; pick heads with some length of stem in midsummer when they show good color but before they get too ripe; hang in bunches in a dry, airy spot out of direct sun. Wild white yarrow is better left until fall when it dries on the plant. Then hang in bunches; it provides a good brown note.

Primarily for Seed Pods

The flowers of all the plants listed below are good garden decoratives, but our primary concern is with their interesting seed vessels. Those marked * can be picked just as the seeds are ripening but while the pods are still green for an interesting variation.

Balloon-flower (*Platycodon*): pick this great filler in fall after capsule opens to show star at tip, and dry on a screen.

*Baptisia: the bladderlike pods of all species turn blackish when ripe and last for years. They can be sprayed or gilded too.

Butterfly-weed (*Asclepias tuberosa*): gather pods with stems in fall as soon as they open or even sooner and allow to open completely as they dry upright in jars in an airy spot; don't let them get too weathered, as they lose body quickly outside.

Canna: gather round capsules as they develop, and dry on a screen.

*Columbine (*Aquilegia*): all species have interesting seed capsules; gather before they get weathered.

*Datura: prickly outsides are quite different; small, unripe ones that remain globular are most useful. Mature ones open to show white ribs in the center, but you must carefully remove and dispose of all the seeds, since they are dangerously poisonous.

*Delphinium: always pick green and unopened, since the development of the seed is very hard on the longevity of the plant. Annual larkspur and aconite are similar.

Day-lily (*Hemerocallis*): pick ripe pods after they open in fall.

Flax (*Linum*): rub tiny globes off stem while still somewhat green, and dry on a screen; good fillers.

Gas-plant (*Dictamnus*): pods of this wonderful garden decorative resemble stars; pick when ripe.

Grape-hyacinth (*Muscari*): pick stems with heads after seeds are ripe; good filler in arrangements.

Iris: pick stems with seed heads after dry in fall; Siberian species are especially good.

Martynia or Unicorn-plant (*Proboscidea jussieui*): grow this in an out-of-the-way, sunny corner. To get a big crop, gather pods continually in summer while still green but at least 3 in. long. Leave on a screen in a dry, warm spot until outer husks split off. You can also wait until fall and gather as they dry on the bush, but crop will be much smaller, and larger seed pods are not as useful as smaller ones. Immature ones can be baked for several hours, then left on a screen until absolutely dry. Pods last forever, and black seeds are useful for eyes.

Penstemon: seed heads of all species interesting as fillers; pick after they turn brown in fall.

Peony: pick pods after they ripen in fall.

Plumbago (*Ceratostigma*): pick bristly heads while still green, dry on a screen, spray with glaze to strengthen.

Poppy (*Papaver*): seed capsules of all species good; pick after seeds have ripened. They can either be used whole or in separate pieces; clip off the top to make a flat disk, and keep the rest as is.

Thermopsis: small, gray, furry seed pods make good bunny ears and fillers; pick after completely dry in early fall.

Yucca: seed capsules of all species interesting; pick in early fall after they open; big, black seeds make good eyes, and large pods can be carefully pried apart to make flower designs.

Primarily for Calyxes

Bachelor's-button (*Centaurea*): all species leave interesting calyxes after flowers blow; pick while green. The perennial *C. montana* is even better; gather its seed heads when no longer green but before completely ripe. Dry all types on a screen.

Chinese lantern (*Physalis*): all species have horrible spreading roots, so never grow them in the gar-

Fig. 1-31. Fresh martynia pod on the right will dry and shed its outer husk; the tail will separate as it dries to look like the "bird" on the left.

Fig. 1-32. Large yucca pod was taken apart to form three segments of this focal point on a wreath. Fluffy white trimming is pearly everlasting.

Fig. 1-33. More decorations from the garden, left to right: seed head of perennial bachelor's-button, calyx and immature seeds of stokesia, calyx of coreopsis.

Fig. 1-34. Blackberry-lily got its name from its striking seed. It is a long-lived perennial with orange flowers in midsummer.

den but in a waste spot somewhere. Calyx of *P. francheti* turns red in fall; gather then and hang to dry in an airy spot out of bright light. Common ground cherry dries tan but if gathered early, may stay green; hang in a dry, darkish spot.

Composites: many daisy flowers lose their seeds from the center but retain interesting calyxes. All are worth trying, but the Shasta daisy and the liatris are two good ones if picked while still green and dried quickly on a screen; spray with glaze to strengthen when dry. Coreopsis heads should be picked green and dried in a hot place on a screen. Sometimes they retain a green tint; pick out seeds after drying if you want a cup shape.

Cupid's-dart (*Catanache*): gather grayish calyxes after they dry on plant or cut green, and dry quickly on a screen.

Phlox: the calyx of summer phlox is a tiny star, fragile but lovely when fitted in clusters into arrangements; gather in late fall when dry.

Stokesia: cut while still green but partially developed, and dry on a screen; or gather just as seeds ripen, but these will be quite fragile.

For Special Purposes

Artemisia: species with gray or white leaves are very useful, but all spread rapidly, so place accordingly in a dry, sunny garden. *A. albula* (Silver King) produces great spires; *A. stelleriana*, *A. frigida*, *A. filifolia*, and *A. argentea* are also good. The dwarf Silver Mound is great in the garden but must be pressed if you dry it. Pick the others toward the end of summer when flower buds have swelled out but before they actually open. They will wilt if picked too early; if picked too late, they may mold or lose their good gray color. Hang most of the crop upside down in bunches in a dark corner; put others upright in jars or around a log to get graceful curves. Once they have dried completely (which may take a month), they will keep well for at least a year if protected from dust in a plastic bag. Very dry branches can be made more pliable by hanging overnight in a humid bathroom with the door closed.

Blackberry-lily (*Belamcanda*): this relative of the iris bears sprays of orange lilylike flowers in mid-summer. Allow seeds to develop until outer husk just begins to peel; cut with long stems, and dry upright in an airy, warm spot. Husk opens to reveal a "blackberry" of seeds very effective in dried arrangements. Spray with insecticide as soon as husk opens.

Honesty (*Lunaria*): biennial easily grown from seed. Don't pick purple flowers the second year; they will develop into large, papery, silver disks; pick as soon as they begin to dry on the plant, keep upright in a jar in an airy spot until completely desiccated, and they will store for years.

Quaking grass (*Briza maxima*): heads resemble sea oats. Sow seeds annually in full sun; pick some green, let others turn tan. Dry upside down in small bunches; spray with insecticide when ready.

From Fields and Roadsides

Nature provides raw materials in infinite abundance along roadsides and in abandoned corners for those who are smart enough to harvest them. I must remind you that all land belongs to someone, and there are laws of trespass. You will never, of course, pick in parks or sanctuaries. If you want a yield for future years, take time to shake the seeds from the pods you gather to assure another generation of plants. Over-picking will wipe out wild plants as quickly as the bulldozer and asphalt. Nothing on this list, to my knowledge, is an endangered species, but that doesn't mean it couldn't become one. Many of today's rare wildflowers were once common, victims of man and his machinations. The really garden-worthy ones are listed above in that section rather than here to encourage you to plant them. The following are readily obtainable and well worth the trouble:

Aster: gather heads in late fall after winds have cleaned the flowerlike calyxes; delicate fillers.

Bladder-nut (*Staphylea*): shrub usually found in moist spots; bears three-lobed pods in fall.

Cattails: found in wet places; gather immature ones early in summer and place upright in jars to dry; brown ones picked in early fall should be sprayed with glaze to prevent shattering.

Club and Spike mosses (*Lycopodium* and *Selaginella*): many species like ground pine were once used to make wreaths and roping and are now very scarce in many places. I disapprove of gathering them for this purpose, unless you also propagate them actively; they are lovely, however, in places where they can root.

Dock: amazingly sturdy roadside and garden weed; gather wands of seeds at different times after they develop to obtain various colors from chartreuse to rust, and hang upside down to dry.

Eupatorium: this genus includes joe-pye weed, mistflower, boneset, and white snakeroot. Flower heads gathered before they open can be dried on a screen for interesting fillers; spray afterward with glaze to strengthen.

Evening primrose (*Oenothera*): roadside weed; tall biennial species are best sources of seed capsules, which look like hyacinth florets. Gather branches in early winter when they are dry and open; soak overnight if necessary to make them pliable for wreaths.

Fern fronds: some ferns bear decorative, fertile spikes; gather in late fall after spores have been released.

Golden alexander (*Zizia aurea*): yellow flower that resembles Queen-Anne's-lace; found in moist places; pick when entirely open, and press or hang upside down to dry in a darkish, airy spot; good filler.

Goldenrod (*Solidago*): genus containing dozens of species. Gather flowers before they are entirely open to use in wreaths; dry seed heads in late fall may be sprayed green to make miniature trees; stem galls also interesting.

Grasses: leaves and stems of all sorts of wild grasses from the wiry fingers of crab grass to the rare sea oats can be utilized; gather while still green, and hang in bunches upside down to dry. Spray with insecticide before bringing indoors.

Lichens: crustose and foliose types include some interesting growths often found on rocks and trees, which can be scraped off with a knife and dried on a screen; fruticose lichens, such as British soldiers, pixie cups, and spoon lichens, are great for miniatures, but dry on a screen first. Gray reindeer moss of colder regions makes a wonderful filler, as does chartreuse lichen from the West Coast.

Mallow (*Malva*): gather round seed capsules in summer while still green, dry on a screen, then spray with glaze.

Milkweed (*Asclepias*): of the weedy milkweeds, the most useful is the large-podded variety found on roadsides and in fields; gather in fall while still green but nearly ripe so pods split easily. Remove silk and seeds carefully, and stuff pod with tissue so it will dry evenly on a screen; hold pod together with a rubber band while drying if you want it closed. Soak old pods overnight in warm water to make them pliable; soak discolored pods several days in a strong solution of chlorine bleach and water to whiten them. Dry silk can be stored indefinitely in a plastic bag.

Morning glory (*Ipomoea* and *Convolvulus*): the beautiful wood rose often offered for sale is a member of this family; seed capsules of the lesser relatives, if gathered while green in summer and dried on a screen, sometimes retain their color and resemble rosebuds; also pick in fall when they turn brown. Capsule inside the flower is less fragile than sepal covering.

Moss: sphagnum moss gathered green from swamps can be used in many projects; stays wet for many months if kept in a plastic bag in a cool place; you can also dry well on a screen and spray green. Many other mosses can be gathered and dried for various uses. Packages of mixed dried varieties can be purchased.

Mountain mint (*Pycnanthemum*): gather flower heads in summer before completely open and dry on a screen or hang upside down in an airy spot, or gather brown seed heads in fall; filler material.

Mullein (*Verbascumthapsis*): biennial weed found on dry roadsides. Gather furry, gray leaves in spring or fall before badly eaten; press large individual leaves; dry whole small rosettes on a screen. Brown heads of seed capsules in fall also interesting but must be treated with insecticide.

Mushrooms: extreme care must be taken when dealing with this tribe, for many of the prettiest are terribly poisonous. If in doubt, leave it alone, and always wash your hands very well after handling. Never leave around where small children may get at them. Many of the soft mushrooms, if gathered

Fig. 1-35. Assorted grasses picked at the edge of the garden were dried upside down for later use.

Fig. 1-36. Arum lily made from a dried milkweed pod glued to a straight woody stem. The center is a seed pod of self-heal, glued on to hide the stem joining..

Fig. 1-37. Black walnut indicates the size of this huge mushroom found dried and intact in my backyard. It may be a puffball caught by early freeze.

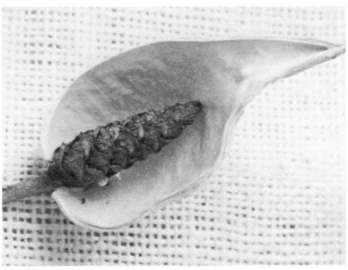

31

Fig. 1-38. Pieces of shelf mushroom taken from an old log in the garden and washed carefully.

Fig. 1-39. A flower made of small pieces of shelf mushroom glued together; artificial berries hide the center joining.

before they are completely ripe, can be dried successfully if you do it quickly in a slow oven, on top of the furnace, or on a screen in hot sun. Little ones come in very handy for miniatures. The so-called shelf mushrooms, which are projections on trees and logs, are much safer and come in many different colors; gather in fall, wash gently if dirty, and dry on a screen as quickly as possible. Little puffballs, if picked before ripe, can be dried the same way. You can also buy dried mushrooms at the grocery; these are edible, so you can use them with impunity for decorations.

Pepper-grass or Pepperweed: these members of the mustard family, which have round, flat seed capsules, should be gathered in spring while still green and hung upside down in a dark corner to dry.

Queen-Anne's-lace (*Daucus carota*): pick white flowers in early summer before completely out; press or hang upside down in a dark corner, depending on intended use. If you plan to dye them, pick in late bud stage, and insert in jars of water with a strong solution of food coloring; as soon as flowers show color, press or hang as above.

Rabbit-foot clover (*Trifolium arvense*): gather soft, pinkish-silver heads in sunny waste places in summer before they are quite open; then hang to dry or use immediately in wreaths; they also press well.

Reeds (*Phragmites*): these grow in moist spots; seed heads resemble plumes. Gather in late summer or early fall before completely dry, then hang in bunches upside down or stand upright in jars in a warm spot; spray with glaze to strengthen when dry.

Rose mallow (*Hibiscus*): often found in moist spots; gather dry seed capsules in late summer or early fall.

Sea-lavender (*Limonium vulgare*): a plant of the salt marshes. Gather branches in summer before all flowers are completely out, and hang in bunches to dry in a dark corner.

Seaweed: if dried carefully in the sun, many varieties can be used to lighten an arrangement of seashells.

Sedge (*Carex* and *Cyperus*): often found in moist spots; gather before heads completely out and hang in bunches to dry.

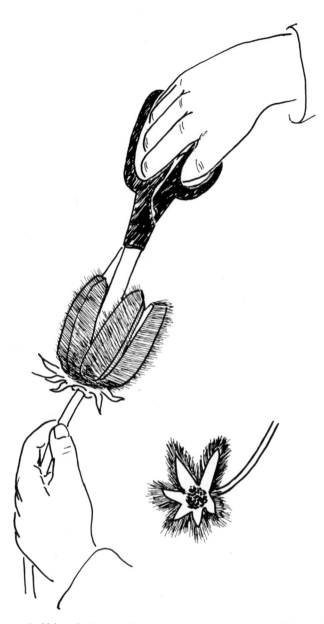

Drawing 3. Old teasels make the easiest flowers. Cut the pod almost in half vertically with scissors, then trisect each half almost to the bottom of the pod. Dip a hemlock cone in glue, and force it down into teasel to hold the petals apart. A small nut or strawflower can be substituted for the cone.

Thimbleweed (*Anemone* and *Geum*): several species of these genera bear small, bristly, round seed heads, which are much nicer to deal with than those from burdocks. Gather while still green, dry on a screen, and spray with glaze.

Thistle: old, spent thistles gathered in late fall can be used to give flower effects; if picked earlier, just as the down begins to fluff, spray top heavily with clear glaze, and leave to dry on a screen. Buds picked green and just as purple appears at tips can be dried on a screen and often retain color; leaves press well. Big bull thistle is a biennial worth cultivating in an odd spot; goldfinches delight in its seed. Canadian thistle is an obnoxious weed, but its heads and those of many related wild companions make good fluffy accents once they are set with spray glaze.

White campion (*Lychnis alba*): small, round capsules ready in late summer and fall; gather before they weather too much.

Wild lotus and Spatterdock (*Nelumbo* and *Nuphar*): seed capsules of true water lilies develop underwater, but the fruits of these two companions are often found above the surface of ponds in late fall; gather on stems, and dry upright in jars.

Wild senna (*Cassia*): small, brown pods ready early in fall.

Sources of Supply

No matter where you live or how provident you are at recycling, there will be some supplies and raw materials that you must buy. Your local florist is the first place to visit. He will be able to suggest other places nearby where you may find what you want. I have two excellent supply houses, but neither does mail-order business, and this is typical of the trade. Ads in garden magazines may guide you to other sources, but the following businesses have mail-order lists worth your while:

Junior's Plant Shop
Glen St.
Rowley, Mass. 01969

Squirrel's Delight
205 Mesinger Ave.
Modesto, Cal. 95350

The Marketplace
141 Dunning Ave.
Auburn, N.Y. 13021

Sun-Kempt
P. O. Box 231
Yorkville, N.Y. 13495

Self-heal (*Prunella vulgaris*): gather seed heads, preferably just after flowers are out, and dry on a screen.

Teasel (*Dipsacus*): large, prickly seed heads of this biennial last indefinitely, but the nicest ones are those gathered in summer while still greenish yellow; old, weathered ones can be cut to form unusual flowers, as illustrated in Drawing 3, or the pods can be cut horizontally to form interesting disks. Stems have nasty bristles, so use gloves or rub the bristles off before handling.

2
more than a dozen dried wreaths

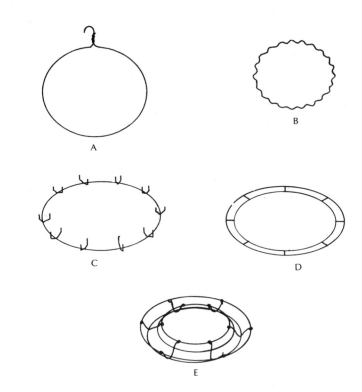

A

B

C

D

E

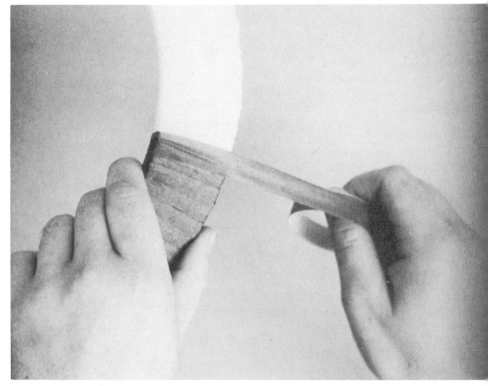

Drawing 4. Common frames for wreaths.

Fig. 2-1. First step for any wreath made on a flat
Styrofoam base is to wrap the form with
overlapping layers of floral tape.

Of all the decorations associated with Christmas, none is more traditional than the wreath. It is really a shame we do not use them in our homes all year round. In earlier times garlands were used for all kinds of festivities. Wreaths have been preserved in Egyptian tombs many thousands of years old, and it is likely that the custom was an ancient one even then. So when you make a wreath today, you have every justification for feeling at one with a long line of human predecessors. We cannot say that they were all peaceful men, but for every laurel wreath given to a victorious war hero, surely a dozen lovers have made garlands or chaplets for their returning sweethearts.

Most of the wreaths that I will be describing are intended to be hung either by themselves or with greens. Many of them are just as effective as a table or sideboard decoration. Here again you can back them with greens, or you can use them as an interesting ring to surround candles, a special statue, or a bowl of fruit or flowers. Smaller sizes are often more in keeping with candles; they are handled separately in Chapter 6, partly because the techniques are slightly different.

There is certainly no good reason why you can't adapt one of these wreaths as a chaplet to adorn the head of your own champion, a birthday child, or a sweetheart. As always, my hope is that you will use the ideas here to create something that is essentially one-of-a-kind, because you made it with your own imagination and materials.

Frames

Drawing 4 shows some frames commonly found at florist supply shops, except for Frame A, which is made from nothing more than a carefully bent metal coat hanger. All of them are used for making wreaths of greenery, as detailed in the next chapter. Frames A, B, and E, however, are sometimes called for in this chapter too. Type E is very strong and is recommended for outdoor wreaths such as the one shown in Fig. C-7, where pine cones are wired rather than glued on to make the wreath waterproof. Frames A and B are most useful for making wreaths of dried materials such as artemisia, hydrangea, and the like

by the continuous wiring method explained later in this chapter.

Lacking any wire at all, you can still make a very satisfactory frame with long, slender, green wands cut from a willow tree. The supplest varieties are best, and thinner sections are the easiest to work with successfully. (The weeping willow is made-to-order for this.) Simply bend a cut withe into a circle of the size desired, and begin winding the thin end back on the thicker part. When you have about 2 in. of withe left, reverse its direction again, and bend it back under the previous winding. Now wind another length around the first, starting and ending at a different point on the circle than before. I usually use three withes per frame, and then I take some very slender pieces about 1 ft. long and add a few extra windings here and there for extra stability. Always bend the loose end back into the previous winding; the pressure holds the last bit of withe in place, just as in tying knots. These frames dry very well, and can even be used over another year. They are especially handy for making small frames, which are not usually sold. Wired items stay in place, because the frame is not slippery.

Many of the wreaths in the first part of this chapter are made on Styrofoam frames. I prefer the flat Styrofoam ring, which is available everywhere in many sizes in November, and at other times in craft shops. A ring with a diameter of 12 in. is the most useful. The ring itself should be about 1¼ in. wide. You can also cut your own ring out of a large piece of Styrofoam with a very sharp, thin, serrated knife or a coping saw. Use a sheet of Styrofoam ½–¾ in. thick.

For wreaths larger than 8 in. in diameter, a backing of corrugated cardboard is a wise precaution. Cut it the same size as the Styrofoam ring, glue the two together, and weight them down overnight. Even stronger is a base cut from thin plywood. For any wreath more than 16 in. in diameter, the wooden base is quite imperative, because the weight of the cones and nuts attached to it becomes too much for the Styrofoam to support. Some artisans make glued wreaths with just flat plywood frames, but I find that these do not have enough depth. It is much better to glue a matching Styrofoam ring to the plywood.

Before you start to decorate any ring, wrap it all around in overlapping layers with floral tape to give it added strength (see Fig. 2-1).

There is another kind of Styrofoam base, which looks a bit like a life preserver. One of its sides is flat, the other rounded. This base is fine for greenery or dried materials attached with floral pins, but I do not like it for gluing purposes.

Backgrounds

Many of the wreaths that I am going to describe can be hung just as they are or with the addition of a bright bow. Some, like very flat heritage wreaths, in Chapter 4, are more effective if they have a background of greenery. Others look best against a slightly larger circle of cardboard covered with colored foil, paper, velvet, or some other striking material that suits your indoor color scheme. Hang the cardboard circle behind the Styrofoam wreath; you may want to cut it a few inches larger than the wreath so that it protrudes slightly on either side.

Heritage Wreath

Materials:
    Styrofoam ring 8–16 in. in diameter
    corrugated cardboard ring (optional)
    white glue and dip pot
    floral tape
    wire for hanger in back
    assorted cones, pods, nuts, and seeds
    clear glaze spray

Whoever coined the term *heritage wreath* wasn't exaggerating; with reasonable care a well-made wreath of this kind will last all your life. It is a lovely gift, and if it is wrapped well in tissue paper and a heavy-duty box, it can be mailed safely. Whether you make it for yourself, for your children, or for a friend, it will be memorable, because you put something of yourself into it. At least some of the decorations will have special significance, reminders of where you gathered them or who gave them to you.

Because of the infinite variety in nature, each wreath is unique. Even when I have made several with the same components and design, each has come out

slightly different. Where you live and vacation will determine what your wreath will be like. If you spend much time at the seashore, you can fashion a wreath of shells and other durable forms of marine life. The basic steps are the same, but remember that shells weigh more than pine cones; you must back the Styrofoam form with cardboard or plywood, even for a small wreath.

Since most of us live inland, it is easier to accumulate cones and nuts, and so the basic techniques I describe feature those raw materials. Chapter 1 contains much information on gathering and preparing these items. Thumb through it for ideas if you have not yet assembled a good collection. It also describes the dip pot, which is almost indispensable for making an indoor heritage wreath.

You can use white glue for any indoor article, but it is not waterproof. If your wreath is to go out in the elements, you are better advised to make a wired one as described at the end of this chapter. You can also use linoleum paste, but unfortunately this dries a dark color and becomes brittle with age. I do not recommend it for indoor decorations.

There are many ways to hang a wreath. I have even used an old curtain hook, but the following is the most adaptable and the easiest. Before you begin to decorate the wreath, wind a piece of flexible wire completely around the form at the point which will be the center top, and twist it at the back so it will stay in place. Allow enough wire to leave 3–4 in. free at the back on each end for future fastening. If you are gluing very light materials on just the Styrofoam ring without additional backing, glue a small piece of cardboard under the front and back of the hanger to prevent it from cutting into the soft ring.

The next step is to trim the outer and inner edges of your wreath. Four materials are perfect for this. The most beautiful but hardest to get are European beech burrs. When fresh, they are a light golden tan, and they open to a lovely flowerlike form. To fasten these, you merely dip the sharp stem of the burr into the glue, and push it into the Styrofoam. Put them closely together all around the edges of the wreath.

Easier to obtain and equally effective for this operation are hemlock cones, spruce cones about 1 in.

Fig. 2-2. Pins help to hold edge trimmings until glue sets. Always remove within 24 hours.

Fig. 2-3. Making a heritage wreath. a. Trimming the edges with halves of sweet-gum balls and half-open European beech burrs. b. Gluing large items on in a concentric circle design. c. Filling in with smaller items. d. Finishing off the wreath with sprigs of pearly everlasting. e. Closeup of wreath features paulownia pod halves, spruce cones, Douglas fir cones, acorn cups, and hemlock cones.

long (black and red, for example), and sweet-gum balls. The latter are easier to use if they are cut in half first. This is handily done with tin snips, wire cutters, or even heavy scissors if the balls are dry. (Fresh balls are very hard to cut.) Glue the balls to the Styrofoam on their flat side.

You can either do about a third of the wreath edge in one sitting and leave it propped to dry before completing, or you can dip each cone in the glue so that one side is well moistened, then fasten it to the side with a straight pin. These pins, incidentally, should be removed within 24 hours, or it becomes very difficult not to pull off the cone with the pin (see Fig. 2-2).

If I am making several heritage wreaths, I try to do all the edges first. By the time I'm finished with the last, the edges of the first will be dry enough to go on to the next step. Trim the inner edge before the outer so you don't have to rest the ring on a trimmed edge. You may be tempted to make a wreath without this prior trimming, but even though the material on the flat side of the wreath almost hides both inner and outer edges, the whole will have greater depth and beauty if you do not leave out this step. Use your oldest, least beautiful cones for the trimming if you don't have a large supply. This edge trimming also adds 1–2 in. to the final diameter of the wreath, and this is usually more pleasing to the eye because the commercial Styrofoam rings are rather narrow.

Having trimmed the sides of the rings, you can now get down to the actual wreath. Even the most experienced craftsman finds it best to arrange the available materials in a rough pattern first to make sure that there is enough of any one item to go around. An easy design for your first attempt is concentric circles of the same cone, pod, or nut (see Fig. 2-3). Or you can repeat a pleasing combination all around the circle. Very round items will sit better if you gently make a small indentation in the Styrofoam with your finger before you glue them in place.

A three-dimensional wreath is more interesting than a flat one. To obtain this effect, use thick materials in the center and smaller ones towards the edges. Or you can glue a first layer of imperfect items on the base to give more height, then build over that after

Fig. 2-4. Bold heritage wreath design made by alternating tops and bottoms of the same kind of pine cone. Focal point on top was necessary, because the pattern did not come out evenly in the space available.

Fig. 2-5. Big satin bow gives a finishing touch to this heritage wreath. A flat wreath of greenery can be placed behind it.

the glue dries. I usually choose something fairly large and substantial for the basic design. The center of the wreath shown in Fig. 2-4 is made of large Austrian pine cones with every other one upside down. This is a pleasing kind of pattern; you can just as easily alternate pine cones and large milkweed pods placed pointing toward the outer edge. In other words, there are no hard and fast rules of design composition.

After gluing down the basic pattern, you must fill it in with little things to gain a finished effect. The most beautiful wreaths are those in which no chink of the frame shows. Remember the watchword: fill in the interstices! Make sure each item has a good supply of glue on its bottom and fits nicely into the chink. This glue dries clear, so don't worry about a little showing.

I have already emphasized the point that small items are much more useful than giants. You will want some variation too in color, texture, size, and shape. A bag of mixed nuts from the grocery may be a helpful purchase. Brazil nuts, pecans, and filberts are particularly interesting. Empty halves of English walnuts and almonds can be used without any wastage at all. Make sure while you are gluing the nuts that part of them will show when you're finished. I often let the nuts poke just slightly beyond the edge trimming so they will be noticed.

You can obtain different effects from the same item merely by gluing some on edge and others at an angle; prop them up until the glue dries. Cones can be cut in half either vertically or horizontally for still another appearance. Naturally, for a lasting decoration like this, use only the cleanest raw materials. Check Chapter 1 for hints on how to treat dirty or old items.

You can buy or make painted cones and pods, but somehow these lose their natural charm. I prefer a wreath in natural shades. Once all the glue is dry, spray the whole wreath twice with clear glaze as a preservative. You'll be surprised at how this extra sheen emphasizes the natural colors. A few strawflowers, pearly everlasting, statice, tiny bows of bright ribbon, or some gilded holly leaves can be worked into the wreath while you are gluing to add a bit of contrast (see Fig. 2-6).

Variation: a very large heritage wreath is an absolutely gorgeous decoration for the focal point in a room. To make such a giant, first cut a circle of the desired size from a large sheet of wrapping paper. A homemade compass is easy to construct with a thumbtack, a pencil, and a length of string, as shown in Drawing 5. This gives you a perfect circle of whatever size you decide is appropriate. Depending on the diameter of the circle, the final ring should be at least 2 in. wide for a large wreath. The second circle, which determines the size of the ring, is also drawn with the compass. Once you are sure the paper ring is the right size, transfer it to plywood with carbon paper.

After you have cut the plywood ring, make a series of suitable arcs from a large block of Styrofoam 1 in. thick, and fit them around the wooden form in a continuous ring. Glue these well to the wood, and weight the entire ring overnight. (Books are great for this.) Then wrap the ring completely with floral tape before you begin the wreath. The Styrofoam adds depth to the wreath, which is after all a rather monumental piece.

This wreath can accommodate much larger items than a smaller one. The big pods of *Magnolia grandiflora*, whole lotus and waterlily pods, clusters of nuts, martynia pods, even whole long pods from the honey locust tree are possibilities. Place some of them so they overlap the edges of the ring a little to give a bit of irregularity to the huge circle. (I have assumed that you trimmed the inner and outer edges as a preparatory step.) At most such a wreath needs only some ribbon to complete the picture. A big bow of wide ribbon placed on top of the wreath with long streamers falling behind into the empty space in the center is very effective.

You will need a large quantity of smaller things to fill in around and between the larger items in a wreath this size. Start collecting them well ahead of time. You will have a breathtaking heirloom when you finish. Give it at least three coats of clear glaze spray on separate days. Over the years a cone or two may fall off, but it is easy either to reglue or to replace with something else. Always store the wreath in a plastic bag with mothballs to discourage wildlife.

HOMEMADE COMPASS

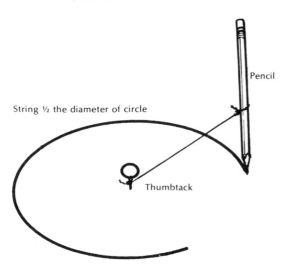

String ½ the diameter of circle

Pencil

Thumbtack

Fig. 2-7. Small leaves of evergreen magnolia have been fitted together to make this wreath. Finished version with sprigs of pearly everlasting and a fancy bow is shown in Fig. C-15.

Fig. 2-8. Larger leaves and a different pattern make a completely different magnolia wreath.

If this wreath appeals to you, my advice is to wait a year or so before making it, meanwhile filling a special box with items just for it.

Magnolia Leaf Wreath
Materials:
  Styrofoam ring at least 12 in. in diameter
  corrugated cardboard ring (optional)
  dried leaves of *Magnolia grandiflora*
  cotton
  floral tape
  white glue and dip pot
  assorted small dried materials

This beauty is really only a variation on the heritage wreath, but it requires a different technique and imparts an airier effect. It can be displayed at the beginning of fall or even used all year in a room featuring browns, greens, or other warm autumn colors. Men are often quite taken with this wreath.

Since the finished wreath is very light in weight, it is not necessary to back the Styrofoam ring, but you may wish to anyway just to ensure that the ring will not break after all your work. (This has happened to me, and the glue held everything together; only the Styrofoam broke. I was able to glue it back together, and then I added cardboard braces on the back over the breaks. This convinced me to take the extra time to put cardboard backings on all my future wreaths.)

Chapter 1 tells you how to gather and dry the magnolia leaves. If you do not have access to this southern tree, you can buy leaves, but the prices are steep. I advise this wreath only for those who live where the tree grows.

Smaller leaves are easier to work with than larger ones if you are gathering your own. It took nearly three dozen medium-sized leaves to make the wreath in Fig. C-15. The wreath in Fig. 2-8 is made with bigger leaves and appears to require less, but actually parts of the leaves are cut off, so you still need several dozen. The tops of all leaves that you use must be perfect.

Don't get discouraged when you start one of these wreaths. It is not easy, but it is worth the extra effort. Even though you improve with practice, no one com-

Fig. 2-9. The ends of these leaves have been trimmed to make them fit better. This wreath is being made in two directions, as described in Drawing 7.

Fig. 2-10. A piece of cotton helps to hold glue and leaves together on the form.

pletes it in a single sitting. As a preliminary, the ring is wrapped in floral tape and the edges are trimmed just as with the heritage wreath.

I begin the leaf placement by sorting through those in my collection until I have a large, flat box cover full of leaves of the same size. This allows you to see what leaves you have available and to look them over constantly. One reason why this wreath is so lovely is that the leaves curl as they dry, but this compounds the difficulty in gluing them on the ring. I usually take a couple at a time and try to see how they will fit together. This is necessary whether you are making a wreath where the leaves are more or less glued on in pairs or one where a single leaf overlaps another. There is always some variation in color too. Some may dry green, others in shades of orange or yellow, and the bulk in browns. I try to space the odder-colored ones out around the ring as I work.

As you can see in Figs. 2-9–2-11, you can make the job a bit easier by trimming off part of the stem end of each leaf as you see how it's to fit. A small ball of cotton is dipped in the glue pot, and then whirled around so both top and bottom are covered. This supports the leaves in place and adds strength to the wreath. No cotton shows when you look directly at the wreath, but in Fig. 2-11 you can see that if someone peered directly at the side of the wreath, he could see it inside doing its job. Some leaves are curved and sized so that they will slip right into position without trimming or cotton, but I give each a wisp of cotton anyway as an anchor.

Often I will glue down a few inches of leaves and then weigh that much down with something not too heavy until the glue dries. The leaves tend to be supple, so they will stay flatter after the glue has dried if so weighted than if simply left as they fit. Making the leaves overlap and curve interestingly from side to side is part of the charm of the magnolia wreath. It is easier to make one where big leaves overlap each other than one where smaller leaves are fitted together, but the latter is daintier.

If you have only a few good leaves, you can make a wreath where you work them into the design of cones and pods, but here they will be prone to damage, because any leaves that protrude much are apt to

Fig. 2-11. Cotton hidden beneath leaves gives added strength and doesn't show, except to the inquisitive camera taking a side view.

Fig. 2-12. Giant allium seed head with a strawflower glued to its center decorates a bow made from large magnolia leaves. A few small yellow and red starflowers lighten the brown circle of medium-sized magnolia leaves.

break with time. It is better to lay the leaf flat on top of a nut or something without sharp edges as a prop, then fill in around them so that only part of the leaf finally shows.

You may be tempted to try this wreath with other kinds of magnolia leaves, but they do not work too well. The great southern magnolia is an evergreen; its leaves have a body that the others in the genus lack, especially if gathered before they have weathered much. The undersides of many have a rusty, furry surface; you can use them backwards for a change of pace.

Usually I add something to the finished wreath. A few individual sheaves of plain sea oats, sprigs of statice or pearly everlasting, or some strawflowers seem to be perfect final touches. They also hide any tiny discolorations on the leaves. For a more masculine look, glue in some small dark pine cones judiciously here and there. You can fashion a rosette of a few perfect leaves as a focal point at the top or bottom of the wreath, as in Fig. 2-12, but I prefer a bright bow fastened on a long corsage pin, which makes it easy to place wherever you want it.

Before making the bow, give the whole wreath at least two good doses of clear spray. This shiny glaze transforms the dullish dried leaves into a wondrous decoration and also adds considerable strength. Since they are fairly fragile, these wreaths should be stored in a substantial box to prevent crushing. They will then last many years.

Variation: many of the magnolia leaves you pick up will show imperfections after they dry; not breaks but strange colorations. You can still make a really striking wreath from these. Fashion the wreath as above, and then spray it with gold, silver, or pure white paint. With a backing of greens and a bright ribbon bow, this is a gorgeous holiday decoration.

Holly Wreath
Materials:
    Styrofoam ring
    dry holly leaves
    gold or silver paint
    white glue and dip pot
    skewer

Holly is another broad-leaved evergreen with foliage that has plenty of body even after it dries. I have gathered dry leaves from under the tree that have worked beautifully, but the best ones are those that you save as you do your pruning. Toss some of the smaller branches into a basket, and leave them in a warm place to dry; you can even store them in the garage by hanging a bunch of tied branches upside down. The only thing you have to guard against is mold. If you do any pruning in the warm months, spread the leaves out somehow until they are completely dry; they can then be stuffed in a plastic bag until you want them. (Leaves gathered from live pruning often retain a greenish tinge, incidentally.)

You can spray the leaves, but it is very wasteful of expensive paint. I wait for a nice day, spread some newspapers on the floor of the workroom, and gild a whole crop of leaves at one time with an old paint brush. This doesn't take too long, since you only need to paint the outer side of each leaf. The dry leaves take paint very well. They dry in a few hours if well aired, and can then be stored in plastic bags against dust. Often I grade them as I paint into three sizes—small, medium, and large—for later selection. I leave small prunings with only a few leaves as is so I can later apply several leaves to the wreath with one skewering.

I do not cover the Styrofoam ring with floral tape for this type of wreath, because it is much easier to insert the stems of the leaves. Simply take individual leaves or small prunings, dip the stems in glue, and stick them into the Styrofoam. (Preliminary holes made with the skewer are not always necessary.) You can place the larger leaves in the center of the ring and the smaller ones on the sides or just scatter them as they come to hand, but do make sure that you hide the stems of one layer with the leaves of the next. Don't try to take the shortcut of placing the leaves and then spraying the wreath. Without the protection of the floral tape, the Styrofoam will evaporate where the paint hits it. Used against a background of greens, this wreath is a most effective holiday decoration on a wall or surrounding candles on a flat surface (see Fig. 4-7).

American holly is especially good for this kind of work, because the leaves are so typical. Some hybrids may have foliage that is not quite so hollylike, but almost all the evergreen hollies can be used. Small-leaved hollies like the hybrid Blue Girl are very easy to work into mixed wreaths of cones and pods as well.

Unless you have a special reason for using flat leaves, do not press your clippings. The natural curls and curves that result as the leaves dry make the wreath just that much more interesting. You may want to wear light work gloves, for the holly leaves maintain their spines to the bitter end, and you have to get your fingers right in there to stick the leaves close enough together to make the wreath full.

I have never painted holly leaves white, but I think that would make another interesting variation. I do know that painting them green has been disappointing. For some reason they look plastic! An artificial look doesn't bother me with gold or silver paint, because the undersides of the leaves are still greenish.

Artemisia Wreath
Materials:
    coat hanger bent into a circle
    or
    crinkled wire frame
    floral tape
    wands of artemisia, dried or fresh
    spool of thin wire
Even when highly decorated, artemisia wreaths retain a certain subtlety, probably because of the soft gray color of the foliage. The frames suggested are types A and B in Drawing 4. The crinkled wire one is a little easier to use, because the bends in the frame make it less likely that the bunches of foliage will slip as you wire them on, but this is not a crucial point. I like the 8-in. diameter size best, but if you have many artemisia wands, you can make bigger ones. The coat hanger ring usually measures 11–12 in. in diameter. Clip part of the hook off to make it less obvious. You may have to hide the hook with your ribbon bow, but this is easy enough to do. If you choose a hanger made from thinner flexible wire, you can even take it apart to make it smaller. Wrap either frame carefully with floral tape to remove all slip from the wire.

There is a world of difference among artemisias. Some grow in thin spires. A. albula (Silver King),

Fig. 2-13. Gilded holly leaves lighten a heritage wreath.

Fig. 2-14. Large chartreuse pods of wisteria were wired right into this wreath of Silver King artemisia.

which was used for the wreath in Fig. 2-14, is the best of these, but there are several others listed in Chapter 1. Another which is probably *A. stelleriana*, grows in a more graceful, arching fashion. I used it for the wreaths in Figs. C-11 and C-13. The different growth habits of the two varieties make quite dissimilar wreaths.

For wreath work, do not pick your artemisia until sometime in late summer. It is hard to determine the exact moment, but you will be fairly close if you do the picking after the plants bud out but before the rather insignificant flowers are quite open. If you pick them too soon, they tend to wither and flop rather than dry gracefully; if you wait too long into the fall, the foliage may mold on the plant. Until you are sure, it is better to be a little late than too early. You will find, however, that if you wait until the flowers open, the pollen is rather overpowering.

I cut Silver King artemisia in long wands, tie them together, and hang them upside down in my garage to dry. The plant is herbaceous, so it is not harmed by cutting it almost to the ground in the fall. There is enough humidity where I live at that time to keep the foliage from becoming brittle, although it does stiffen some. I sometimes cut my arching artemisia the same way, but I have also cut it in shorter lengths and made wreaths that same day. These wreaths must be set on a flat surface where it is warm and dry for several days to allow the foliage to stiffen in place. Wreaths made with fresh leaves are usually more uniformly round, but you can also get this effect with dried foliage if you use smaller bunches of pieces no longer than 5 in. and wire them closer together. If your dried artemisia becomes too brittle to work with, put the bunches in the bathroom overnight, take a good shower, and close the door after you leave to give them a dose of humidity. This is usually enough to let you work the next day.

The wands of artemisia that carry flower buds are the prime crop. If you have a limited quantity, mix some of the leaved branches with some of the flowered ones in every bunch so that your wreath is uniform. Put one central long piece and several smaller ones on either side of every bunch. About six wands per bunch makes a nice wreath. The larger the

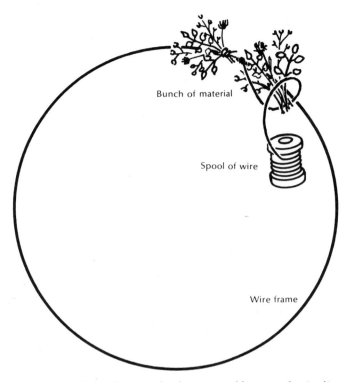

Bunch of material

Spool of wire

Wire frame

Drawing 6. Continuous wiring is the fastest way to make a wreath. In practice, each bunch of material is closer together than this picture indicates. Components were separated to show the process.

to each bunch as that wreath was made up. Choose your technique according to your materials.

Artemisia wreaths stay nice indefinitely, but the color fades after a few years, and in time they get quite dusty. When that happens, unwind the wire, and save it and the frame for a new attempt. Use the old foliage for the next type of wreath.

Artemisia Wreath Base
Materials:

    single wire frame (as for previous wreath)
    stems of artemisia or other foliage
    spool of thin, unpainted wire
    findings of all sorts

Most artemisia is several feet high when fully grown, and you use only the tops of the stems for the previous wreath. The foliage also loses some of its attractive silvery whiteness after a few years. The discarded stems and the old foliage can be used to make a wreath base that can be decorated in different ways to last several more years.

Fasten the wire on the spool to the frame securely. Then simply gather a large bunch of foliage 3–6 in. in length, and bend it around the wire frame where you have secured the wire. Wrap the wire loosely around the bundle every 4 in. or so, adding a new bunch of foliage whenever the previous one runs out until you get all around the frame. To make the final result uniformly fat, work in a few extra branches if necessary. Note that you are not wiring separate small bunches individually as in the previous wreath, but rather you are gathering a lot of loose stems and bending them around the frame. You end up with a grayish base. Almost anything can be stuck into the spaces between the stems.

One simple finishing touch is to wrap thick colored yarn around the wreath, as in Fig. 2-15. Try to keep all the bands the same distance apart. You can also use ribbon or gay strips of cloth in the same way. I had some stray pieces of pearly everlasting that had been sprayed red, so I tucked them between strands of green yarn and added a few sprigs of fresh artemisia around the edges of the ring. In Fig. 2-16 you can see how this transformed the plain base into a totally different wreath.

diameter of the frame, the larger and longer the individual bunches must be. It takes a lot of artemisia to make a good full wreath.

You can wire each bunch on the frame separately, but it is much faster to do continuous wiring (see Drawing 6). Fasten the end of the wire firmly to the frame, then unwind about 1 ft. from the spool. Hold your first bunch of foliage together with one hand while you go around it and the frame twice with the wire and the spool. Don't pull the wire so taut that it cuts the foliage, but do make it tight enough to hold the bunch in place. Put the spool aside, and lay a second bunch of foliage in the same direction as the first so that its decorative end hides the stems of the preceding bunch. Wind the wire and spool around again. Proceed in the same way all around the frame, unwinding more wire from the spool as necessary. On the last bunch, wind the wire around a few extra times, cut it from the spool, and work the end of the wire back so it can't unwind.

You can decorate your artemisia wreaths with other dried items, or you can leave them plain with just a lovely ribbon. The wreath with the yellow strawflowers (Fig. C-12) was made first, and the wired strawflowers were worked in afterwards. The pink heads of the rabbit-foot clover, however, were added

Fig. 2-15. Old wands of artemisia were first wired to the frame loosely to make a base, then covered with thick green yarn wound around in continuous fashion; small pieces of red-dyed pearly everlasting give the wreath extra color.

Fig. 2-16. Small sprigs of fresh artemisia slipped into the base completely transform this door wreath.

Variation: you can use the same technique to make a wreath base of raffia or straw, which can then be decorated any way you wish. The unpainted wire does not show on the gray artemisia, but it does against straw. Hide it with the decorative strips you wind around after the wiring.

Evening Primrose Wreath
Materials:
    single wire frame (as for artemisia wreaths)
    dried stems of evening primrose seed capsules
    floral tape
    spool of thin wire
    assorted dried materials
    clear glaze spray

Evening primrose is a roadside weed that can be gathered in late fall or winter, as detailed in Chapter 1. It stores well, so you can lay in a supply one year to use the next. To make it pliable enough to work into wreaths, let it soak overnight in warm water. If the seed capsules are discolored from the weather, pour some bleach into the soak. They dry a soft tan.

Use stems of varying lengths for each bunch. The number will depend on how full of seed capsules each stem is and how big a wreath you are making, but I can state categorically that you will need twice as many to complete the wreath as you originally estimate. It takes several plants of the bigger-branched species to make even a small wreath. If you run out, leave the wreath to dry as far as it's done. Gather some more stems, soak, and continue from where you left off. It is not necessary to soak the half-completed wreath again.

As always, your first step is to wrap floral tape all around the wire frame. Use the same continuous wiring process as in the first artemisia wreath, laying one bunch of stems on top of the previous bunch. Make sure that the wire remains taut at all times. After the wreath dries out, you can gild or silver it lightly by brushing a paintbrush over the tips of the capsules here and there. Or you can glue small cones and strawflowers between the primrose capsules for a totally different effect. Spray the entire wreath with clear glaze when you have finished.

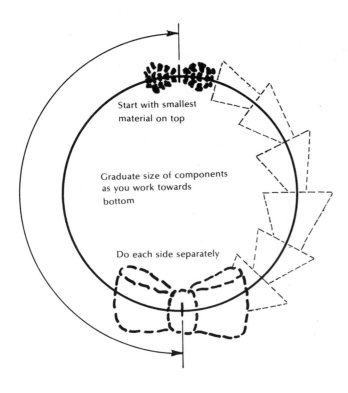

Start with smallest material on top

Graduate size of components as you work towards bottom

Do each side separately

Drawing 7. Two-way wreath is an interesting variation. Divide a circle frame in half, and wire material separately on each portion, starting at the top. Material at the top should be smaller than at the bottom. A bow at bottom center hides the joining.

Hydrangea Wreath

Materials:

    single wire frame (as for artemisia wreaths)
    floral tape
    fresh hydrangea flowers
    spool of wire
    clear glaze spray

This is a fine wreath to display any time, not only on holidays. You can use any kind of hydrangea, as long as it produces good-sized bunches. Use flowers that are still fresh, not dried ones. Gather them at the end of the summer, before the stems have grown brittle; leave about 1–2 in. of stem beneath the flowers and strip off any leaves. Check also for insect life, since spiders love to nest in these flowers. I always shake the bunches as I pick them to get rid of any loose dried flowers as well. Pick bunches of the same size if you can. One really big one is enough for one wired bunch, but you may have to use two or three smaller ones if your supply is limited. You want each layer to be uniform, and the wreath must be good and full to look right.

I prefer the hydrangeas which mature with a pinkish tinge, since I love the combination of pink and cream, but you can just as easily use the blue-flowered types. The latter must usually be gathered a little earlier to preserve some of the blue tint, but the combination of blue and chartreuse often found in late summer can be striking. I have even made a lovely wreath from a bush which had cream flowers variously tinged pink, blue, and green. I tried to turn the bunches to mix the various colors fairly uniformly all around the wreath (see Fig. C-18).

Wrap the wire frame with floral tape, and use the continuous wiring method outlined for the first artemisia wreath. Work with the flowers as soon as they have been picked. Then lay the whole wreath flat in a warm place for several days to dry. You might think that these wreaths would be incredibly fragile, but actually they hold up surprisingly well if you give them a good coat of clear glaze spray after the flowers are dry. The whole trick is to make each bunch that you wire on very full. A bow can be fastened on with wire when you're ready to hang the wreath. I used two shades of soft green to make the bow in Fig. C-18,

Variation: these stems adapt themselves very nicely to the wreath form often depicted on coins. (Drawing 7 shows what I mean.) Again you use continuous wiring for the bunches, but you do it in two different directions, one at a time. Choose branches with smaller and fewer capsules for the first bunch on either side of the center top, and gradually make the bunches larger until you reach the optimum size for good proportion. The joining point of the two sets of stems at the center bottom of the wreath is a natural place to wire on a bow, but you can just as easily hide the raw ends with a little plaque or a rosette made of cones and pods like milkweed. Fig. C-17 shows a combination of these ideas. The gilded plaster angels were bought in the dime store, and the flowers are pink roses made from dyed corn husks. The bow at the bottom is gold and white. What I want to demonstrate is that you can fashion a quite gaudy wreath with as simple and rather plain base as primrose stems. They were left natural to contrast better with the bright angels, but they were given a coat of spray glaze. The soft tan of the dried primrose capsules combines very well with yellow and orange straw-flowers and with chartreuse lichen.

Fig. 2-17. The flat-topped species of goldenrod does not make as full a wreath as the plumy type. A few sprigs of gray artemisia add contrast. A big green satin bow will go at the bottom.

and they complemented the colors of the flowers very nicely. Once the flowers are dry, you can also spray this wreath almost any color, either solidly or preferably in spritzes here and there.

Variation: using one of the life-preserver Styrofoam frames described at the beginning of this chapter or even a flat Styrofoam ring, you can make a different kind of hydrangea wreath. Again, gather the flowers before they get too dry. Use floral pins (see Fig. 1-7) to fasten good-sized bunches of flowers to the Styrofoam. Put the pin through the lower part of the flowers rather than just around the stems. For best results stick a large bunch in the center of the ring and two smaller ones on either side for each layer as you progress around in one direction. Each layer hides the stems of the preceding one. Hang the wreath in a dry place for a few days to prevent mold from developing.

A wreath made in this way is usually fatter and fuller than the wired kind previously described. If you want a large wreath, this is the better technique. The floral pins are expensive, but they are a one-time investment. In a pinch you can substitute good quality, straight hairpins. When the wreath is past its prime, discard the flowers and save the pins and the frame for another time.

You can, of course, insert other kinds of dried flowers in this wreath as you stick the bunches in, which gives still another effect. Or you can wait until the hydrangea flowers are completely dry, then spray splotches of gold paint on the wreath irregularly to liven it up. This is a good idea for older flowers or for hydrangeas that have turned a uniform cream color. After the paint dries, give the whole wreath a thorough coat of clear glaze spray to add strength.

Goldenrod Wreath

Materials:
   single wire frame (as for artemisia wreaths)
   short sprays of fresh goldenrod
   floral tape
   spool of wire
   clear glaze spray
   yellow floral spray (optional)
   assorted dried materials (optional)

Here is another wreath that makes a fine autumn decoration. The secret is to gather the goldenrod flower heads before they are quite open, then make the wreath immediately. As the flowers dry in the wreath, additional florets will open. If you wait until the flowers have matured in the field, your wreath will lose much of its color as it dries. You can gather the heads and hang them in bunches or lay them flat in baskets in the garage for a day or two, but no longer; they quickly get brittle.

Shake the heads very well while you are gathering them, for all sorts of insects, particularly hornets and bees, dote on this flower. I once sat under a tree to make up a wreath as I gathered the flowers, and the incoming hornets flew right onto the wreath itself. Be warned too that it takes a tremendous quantity of flowers to make even a small wreath. You can use the goldenrods which have flattish heads, but the ones that bear their flowers in a plumy inflorescence make the prettiest wreaths.

Proceed as with the hydrangea wreath, cutting off all but 1–2 in. of the stems, trimming off any old flowers, and using a generously fat bunch for each wiring. Hang the completed wreath in a dry place or

Fig. 2-18. Bunches of mixed dried materials were too small and wired too far apart in this wreath. As the items dried, the wreath developed a hungry look.

lay it flat on a screen for a few days, then spray with clear glaze to strengthen it. The yellow color darkens somewhat with age. If it gets too rusty-looking, use some yellow floral spray as a touch-up.

You can intersperse some gray artemisia foliage or some dried strawflowers to liven up the wreath. You can also add a bow or wind a flat ribbon continuously around the whole wreath for a change of pace, as with the second artemisia wreath. This wreath should not be placed where it may easily be brushed against, because goldenrod becomes very brittle. With a bright orange or green ribbon, it makes a striking decoration against a dark-paneled wall. I have seen one which had hung almost a year in such a spot, and it still looked most presentable.

Variation: using the life-preserver Styrofoam ring and floral pins, you can make a goldenrod wreath in the same fashion as with the hydrangeas. Again, this base creates a richer, fuller wreath than the wire frame.

Variation: in like manner, with either a wire frame or the life-preserver frame, you can make dried wreaths out of many other similar raw materials, either singly or in combination. Peppergrass and several other wild mustards, which are common weeds, make very dainty wreaths. Gather them while the seeds are still green and hang in bunches upside down if you're not ready to make your wreath. Soak overnight to make them pliable again. Dried pampas plumes, dock seed heads, and wheat and oat sprays are other good subjects. Some beech and oak trees retain their leaves far into the winter; gather short twigs with these leaves in early fall. You can also work in a stem of baptisia pods or some teasels, pearly everlasting, sourwood seed heads, honesty pods, evening primrose, or iris pods, as well as colored strawflowers. Many of these items are best used while they are still greenish or at least before they are wholly dry. The secret with all of these is to make each bunch of raw materials full and to overlap them closely on the frame. Otherwise you will find that they shrink as they dry further, and your wreath gets a skimpy look, as in Fig. 2-18.

Red Pepper Wreath
Materials:
  flat Styrofoam ring
  floral tape
  long, thin, red hot peppers
  white glue and dip pot
  assorted dried flowers and pods
  clear glaze spray

If you live where hot peppers are widely grown or if your own bushes produce far more than you can use, this wreath is a very different type. It is especially attractive in homes with a Spanish or Mexican flavor, or as a kitchen decoration. Gather the peppers after they have ripened red, and spread them thinly on a screen in the garage to dry. (Do not dry in strong light.) This will take a couple of weeks in the height of summer. You can also hang them to dry in strings, but the stems will shrink; often they will slip out of a knot or break off if you thread them. There are several varieties of hot peppers which are bright yellow at one stage of development. If you pick them then, some will dry with tinges of yellow and orange as well as the more common red.

When the peppers are very dry, they are quite brittle, but they can be glued in place very handily. Wrap your Styrofoam ring in floral tape as previously described for the heritage wreath, but do not bother trimming the edges. Glue the peppers in place so

Fig. 2-19. Magnolia leaves and assorted dried materials were glued to a wicker frame. Red ribbon trimming around the edge is optional.

they more or less go in one direction, and hide the ends of each layer with the next one. Use enough peppers in each layer to hide the ring. Let the peppers stick out over both the outer and the inner edges of the ring for an irregular effect.

The wreath in Fig. C-16 adds dried, yellow tansy flowers to the peppers for a gay color combination. Nuts, dried artichoke globes, yucca pods, artemisia foliage, pearly everlasting, statice, and honesty are other possibilities. Cured correctly, the peppers stay in good shape for years, but a coat of clear glaze spray after the wreath is complete will make dusting easier.

One precaution: these peppers are not called hot for nothing. Even dried, the skins contain a volatile irritating oil. Whenever you handle them, keep your fingers away from your eyes, nose, and mouth, and wash your hands well with several soapings and rinsings afterward. Never leave them within reach of small children.

Wicker Wreath
Materials:
    wicker frame
    white glue and dip pot
    ribbon (optional)
    wire hanger
    cotton
    assorted leaves, cones, pods, etc.
    clear glaze spray

Circles, ovals, and other flat shapes made from woven wicker or similar fibers can be used as bases for all sorts of hanging wreaths. A ribbon in a shade to harmonize with the decor of your home can be woven through the wicker beforehand if you wish.

How you decorate the frame is completely up to you. You'll want some of the wicker to show, but you can glue on a selection of cones and pods around the outer or inner part of the frame, or you can use the frame to set off a dried arrangement like that in Fig. 2-19. I used to fasten the various components to the frame with wire, but glue is much better. If necessary, use some cotton as with the magnolia leaf wreath to help the glued items adhere to the wicker.

Lay out the pattern first to get a good idea of what it will look like, then glue the things in place in layers. If

you are using dried leaves as a background, for example, put them on first. Finish up with some little sprigs of dried material as fillers to hold the design together. When the wreath is complete, give it a good coat of clear glaze spray. This ornament can be hung by itself or against a green wreath. It is usually easy to work the wire for the hanger in after the design is finished. I often use a sling of ribbon instead, working it through an opening near the top of the frame. You can dress up this wreath temporarily by tucking small bits of greenery into the outer edges or on either side of a central design. A small bow with fairly long streamers is another possibility for a finishing touch. It should be obvious that any of these suggestions will work equally well on a three-dimensional wicker object like a basket; just trim the outside and fill the inside.

Outdoor Heritage Wreath
Materials:
    trough wire frame
    spool of wire (gauge 24)
    wire cutter
    assorted cones, nuts, and pods
    clear glaze spray

This chapter ends as it began—with a wreath that will last for many years. One that my clever mother-

in-law made has been in and out of the weather for some ten years and is still going strong (see Fig. C-7). The main difference between the two heritage wreaths is that this one is more or less waterproof, because its components are put together with wire rather than glue. Be forewarned, however, that this does not mean you can blithely put it outside in a downpour. It will come through unscathed, but the cones fold up when wet, and the wreath takes on a very strange appearance until it dries again. You can take advantage of this to make yours last longer. Every few years I put mine out in an early November rain for a thorough soaking, then bring it back into the house to dry for a few days. The cones absorb some of the moisture, and this keeps them from getting too brittle.

The ideal place for this wreath is on a partially protected door, where odd drops of rain and humidity would quickly erode a glued wreath. The wired wreath is particularly good for backing with greens. You can either put a flat wreath of evergreens behind it or insert sprigs of greens between the outer cones to frame it, as in Fig. 2-22.

You can also use a double-wire ring or the chicken wire frame described in Chapter 3 for this wreath, but the trough frame is much stronger and easier to work with. When you are working, its rounded side should be uppermost; this gives the finished wreath a very desirable fullness.

This wreath is perfect for pine cone flowers (see Chapter 1) or for cones which have been cut in half vertically. Any pod which has inherent structural strength (a lotus, for example) can also be utilized, but stay away from very fragile things which might be ruined by strong wind or a good wetting. All sorts of nuts make interesting contrasts; however, you must drill a small hole through the end of each one for the attaching wire. The easiest way to do this is to hold the nut securely in a vise or to have someone else hold it in a nutcracker or pliers while you use a hand drill with a small bit.

Try to gather several different kinds of cones for this wreath. Generally, cones from pine trees hold up better over the years than spruce cones, so use more of them. Small cones like those on Scotch or Austrian pines are good to edge the inner rim of the wreath. You can make as complicated a design or grouping of other types of cones in the body of the wreath as you have raw materials available.

The one secret of success is to make sure that every

Fig. 2-20. Back of a wired heritage wreath showing the frame.

Fig. 2-21. Wired wreath can be displayed with only a big ribbon. This wreath had an outer ring of Norway spruce cones pointing outward when first made ten years ago. They suffered badly in a storm and were never replaced.

Fig. 2-22. Juniper prunings were simply inserted among outsides cones to finish this wreath off. It can also be used with a flat wreath of greenery, as in Fig. C-7.

single cone, nut, or pod is attached to the frame in two places. A trough frame has four rings of strong wire as well as frequent crossbars, so there is ample opportunity to do this. Until you get the hang of how much is needed, cut your pieces of wire a little longer than necessary for each cone. Wind the middle of the piece of wire around the middle of the cone, pull taut, and twist. Then fasten the cone in place by winding either end of the tie wire around different wires of the frame, pulling the tie wires as tight as possible. Needle-nosed pliers are a great help.

Start with the cones for the two edges, and fasten them as closely together as you can. Then you are ready to begin whatever design you have in mind for the body of the wreath. When you are finishing up with clusters of smaller cones or nuts here and there, try to force them down between other larger cones so that they don't flop around. It takes a lot of cones and a lot of work to make this kind of wreath, but it is a job that lasts.

It is worth buying a few special big cones from the West Coast to form focal points on the wreath, as well

as some smaller varieties not native to your area. If you have been collecting some of the bigger cones over the years and have wondered what to do with them, this is your opportunity. Cut some of them across horizontally either with a saw and a vise or with the help of some understanding handy man who owns an electric saw. Use the endmost piece as is, and trim the other portions into flat disks with the wire cutter. Notice how different the backs of many cones are compared with the fronts. Wire some of the cones so their backs face forward, others sideways to get the most interest from whatever raw materials you have at hand.

When you have finally wired in the last cone and have made sure that none of them wiggle, give the whole wreath several coats of clear glaze spray to bring out the highlights. This will also help to keep the cones from folding up in a slight mist. Eventually the wreath will grow old and dry, which indicates that it needs a day out in the rain. When all the components are dry again, apply another coat of glaze.

3
make a tree for indoors

Fig. 3-1. This nut tree is made on a Styrofoam cone form. Note the pins on top, which temporarily hold horse-chestnuts in place until glue hardens.

Mankind has always had a deep affinity with trees. Written history records trees with religious significance among peoples as diverse as the Druids of Britain and the ancient Greeks of the Mediterranean. Earlier still, the Babylonians and the Egyptians pictured trees on their carvings. Rugs from Persia and India bear designs inspired by trees and by the longing of desert people for their beauty and shade.

Our use of Christmas greenery has been attributed to the Roman festival of Saturnalia, but it is more likely that its roots go much further back. Anyone who has suffered from the cold during an energy crisis can easily understand why ancient man was very anxious to make sure that the winter solstice in December was followed by gradually lengthening days. He could take heart then that spring would come as usual.

Whatever the reason, our custom of decorating the house with flowers and greenery in winter is a delight I should not like to give up. While few of us have greenhouses or conservatories, most of us have at least one house plant. At Christmas the Christian goes a step further and actually brings in a real tree. No matter what your religion, you affirm your kinship with the rest of mankind when you make some sort of tree decoration.

It need not be connected with any holiday at all, but it does seem to have more significance in the period between Thanksgiving and Easter or Passover for those of us who live where winter is not green. Depending on what you have available, where you live, and the size of your living quarters, one of the following may be just right for you.

Crab Apple Tree

Materials:
    Styrofoam cone or pyramid 6–8 in. tall
    wooden toothpicks cut in half
    crab apples, hardy oranges, or kumquats
    sprigs of small-leaved greenery
    plate for base

For years it bothered me that no use was ever made of our red crab apples. Season after season the tree produces crops so heavy they bend the branches over. No one ever made jelly, and except for what birds and other wildlife ate, the tree's only contribution was to add to the beauty of the fall.

As you can see in Fig. C-2, crab apples can form just as bright an indoor decoration. This tree can be made anytime after the apples begin to redden. Hardy orange (*Poncirus trifoliata*), a fine ornamental that grows as far north as New York City, kumquats, or any other small fruit that has no real utilitarian purpose can be substituted for the crab apples.

Choose a plate large enough to fit the diameter of the Styrofoam cone plus the size of the apples around it or place on a large tray and surround with greens.

Remove stems and polish fruit before you begin. Sort out the smallest fruits for the top layer. The largest fruits go on the bottom, and this is where you start. Put the pointed end of a toothpick half into each apple, and fasten to the cone by sticking the other end of the toothpick into the Styrofoam at a slight downward angle so that the fruit is held in place by gravity. Go all around the cone before starting the second layer, placing the fruits as closely together as possible. Put the reddest side of the apple outward. The 7-in. pyramid in Fig. C-2 required 54 crab apples; hardy oranges are larger, so only 36 were needed for the same size form.

I filled the interstices between the fruits by pushing tiny Japanese holly sprigs into the Styrofoam. You could use box, privet, or any small-leaved green, even juniper in the far north. The topmost apple was pierced with a skewer to stand a sprig at the very summit of the tree.

I put this tree in the dining room, which is the warmest spot in our house. It was made early in the week of Thanksgiving before the rush of holiday preparation became frantic, and it lasted perfectly until the next weekend, when a few fruits began to brown. They could have been replaced, but instead I threw all the apples into the compost and used the cone again to make a hardy orange tree in the same manner. In a slightly cooler room, it lasted a good two weeks before needing any replacement. These oranges are a yellowish shade, and they have a strong citrus smell which is an added delight. They can also be used for pomanders. As far as I know, that's the extent of their utility.

If you have no source of real fruit, you can get the
same effect by gluing fake fruits on a cone, but at least
use real foliage. You only need a little, since you use
sprigs hardly more than 1 in. long.

I have seen frames made of dowels on which eating
apples, lemons, and other large fruits are stuck to
form a very large fruit tree. This is often advertised as
"in the Williamsburg manner." Although they are
extremely opulent-looking, they are so wasteful.
Unless you can eat the fruit quickly (or make fruit
salad), the warm house conditions will quickly spoil
it, which bothers my Yankee heart. If you want this
kind of effect, why not place some mixed fruits and
nuts in a pretty bowl instead to encourage early
eating?

Nut and Cone Tree
Materials:
    Styrofoam cone
    vintage white glue and dip pot
    straight pins
    assorted nuts, pods, cones, etc.
    clear glaze spray
Closely allied to the crab apple tree, this variation
has the advantage of being nearly indestructible.
Once coated with clear glaze, the finished product
can be stored between uses in a plastic bag with a few
mothballs to discourage insects. Put it in a large tin
can, and not even a mouse can spoil it.

There are several ways to decorate this tree. With a
cone that measures 8 in. or higher, you can use nuts
as the main ingredient and fill the interstices with tiny
pods and cones. With a smaller cone frame, you will
find that only the more diminutive nuts look in scale,
but you can use a combination of nuts and other
natural materials. Make sure that everything is absolutely clean before using.

In either size there are further choices. You can
place straight lines of one type of raw material vertically up and down the form, or you can arrange them
randomly in any order that seems to fit. Although it is
a bit more difficult, the most interesting treatment is
to make spirals of a single kind of nut or cone.

To decorate in this latter fashion, draw a spiral on
the Styrofoam cone with a crayon. It should begin

and end on the same side of the cone. Use this as your guide to glue on the first line of nuts. Grade the nuts first, the biggest for the bottom, the smallest for the top. Begin at the bottom and work upward. This is where the pins come in; before putting a nut in place, make an indentation in the Styrofoam with your finger at the spot where the nut is to go. Dip the nut in the glue, fit it into the indentation, then hold it in place by sticking pins around it. I always use my old glue for this job, because it is much tackier and holds faster. Leave the pins in place until the glue sets well, but don't forget them, since they eventually become quite difficult to remove.

Usually it is not possible to put in more than a few nuts at a time. They are heavy, and even instant-set glue does not hold them immediately. The tree will probably have to be set on its side or cushioned somehow from time to time as you work upward. As one group of nuts sets, add a few more.

A tree made completely of nuts can be quite expensive, and you will want contrasting colors, sizes, and textures to make it interesting. One of the most beautiful that I have ever seen was made of English walnuts, almonds, filberts, pecans, hickory nuts, Brazil nuts, and chestnuts. None of these is cheap, but you get a better bargain if you buy them at the end of the season in spring. Since the tree will be a conversation piece for years, it is easier to justify this than a fruit tree which will rot in a week or two.

The little tree shown in Fig. 3-1 used only waste nuts—acorns, horse-chestnuts, and pig nuts—plus sweet-gum balls, beech burrs, larch cones, and other kinds of pods. Layers of nuts and cones alternate. It involved no expense at all, since I gathered all the items myself. It was also much faster to make, because the spirals of burrs and cones needed less pinning and propping, and they anchored the more difficult nut tiers.

Whatever your combination of raw materials and however you arrange them, the last step is always the same: fill in the interstices with small pods of one sort or another until none of the cone base shows. The filling does not spoil the spiral design, because the fillers are very small in comparison to the strong lines of the larger items. Place a perfect, small pine cone or

suitably shaped nut at the very top. When all the pins have been removed and the glue is well set, give the whole tree several coats of clear glaze, and let it dry well before handling.

This tree can stand alone on a special base, or it can be the focal point of a larger decoration of nuts, fruit, or a few small branches of evergreens, as in Fig. C-10. It mails easily and may well become a treasured part of anyone's traditional trimmings.

Beech Burr Tree
Materials:
    Styrofoam cone 8 in. tall
    white glue and dip pot
    open European beech burrs

This little beauty is merely a variation on the nut tree. I had access to a good supply of the large burrs from an ancient copper beech. A smaller tree could be fashioned from the burrs of the American beech, which are scarcely a quarter the size of the ones I used (see Fig. C-1).

Starting at either top or bottom of the cone, place the burrs as closely together as possible. Make sure they are perfectly clean. Clip off the thin end of the stem, dip the body of the stem in the glue, and stick it into the cone. This tree can be done at one sitting, because the burrs hold each other in place. Spray with clear glaze when finished if you want a shiny effect.

I used to stud this tree with lots of small red rose fence hips (*Rosa multiflora*) and a few sprigs of short-needled pine. The burrs held these temporary decorations in place. Once I stuck tiny glass balls between the burrs.

It began to look a bit shopworn, since several sets of children had played with it, so I finally gave it a coat of green floral spray followed by a few shots of white spray to simulate snow. Then I glued tiny starflowers here and there. It is amazingly treelike in appearance and looks as if it can survive another seven Christmases without difficulty.

Variation: the same basic technique can be used to make a tree entirely from sweet-gum balls, larch cones, or small pine cones. Grade them so that the largest are at the bottom and the smallest at the top. It

Fig. 3-3. Cone made of hardware mesh is the base for this artemisia tree.

Drawing 8. These proportions are the most pleasing to the eye, but they are not always possible. Approach them as closely as you can with the material at hand when making trees in pots or as plaques.

can either be left natural and sprayed only with clear glaze, sprayed green and decorated with tiny flowers or glass balls, or even sprayed gold or silver; all of these are effective.

Artemisia Tree
Materials:
  cone made from ¼-in. hardware mesh
  many branches of tall dried artemisia

To make the hardware mesh cone, proceed as follows: mark a circle 12 in. in diameter on flat mesh with a crayon, cut it out with wire cutters, then cut it in half. Now fold one semicircle into a thinnish cone about 4 in. wide at its bottom, overlapping the mesh as necessary and fastening the outside edge to the cone body with wire at top and bottom (see Fig. 3-3). This cone will make a tree about 15 in. high. If you want a smaller or taller tree, adjust the size of the original circle accordingly.

Since it takes so much artemisia to make a full tree, your supply will determine the size to some extent. For a buffet or mantel, you can actually make only half a tree, since the bare back is placed against the wall.

In either case, start at the top with a long, perfectly formed, branching piece of artemisia. Measure it carefully against the cone, since it will determine the shape and height of the final tree. Trim the leaves from its lower portion, stick it carefully into the top of the cone, and work it down to the bottom. If necessary, tape or wire it to the top of the cone to hold it upright.

Now set up the sides of the tree by working two smaller branches into the bottom of the mesh on either side. Use pieces of artemisia several inches longer than will show on the outside of the mesh; the ends intermingling inside the cone will eventually hold it steadily together. I tend to make my trees too fat by using branches at the bottom that are too long. A thin, tapering tree is the most graceful. Draw an imaginary line from the top of the tree to where the side branches should fit at the bottom. Drawing 8 shows the most aesthetic proportions: come as close to them as you can.

Having established the outline of the tree, you merely fill in between the top and the bottom. The

PROPORTIONS OF POT TO TREE

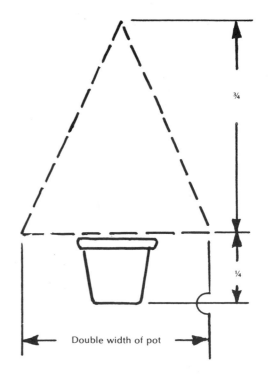

¾

¼

Double width of pot

58

Fig. 3-4. Artemisia tree begins to take shape.

Fig. 3-5. This artemisia tree was deliberately made low and squatty to fit on a table. Christmas balls were later inserted to give color.

easiest procedure is to begin at the bottom; push in more branches the same length as the first two guiders all around. Once this is done, the cone will stand by itself while you work. As you move upwards, make each layer slightly shorter so your tree is pyramidal. Place a few more small branches around the top to make a pleasing transition from the top to the rest of the tree.

Properly dried artemisia (see Chapter 1) is a lovely whitish gray color. It can be decorated in any fashion you like, from tiny red birds to fake pink rosebuds. Or you may put colored glass balls between the branches. The pieces of artemisia tend to hold the decorations on without fancy fasteners.

The bottom of the cone is scratchy, so place it on a plate or tray to protect your furniture. If it is small enough, the base will be completely hidden by the branches. This tree will stay lovely for many months,

but eventually it will grow dusty. You can shake the dust off fairly easily, and I have stored a tree in a plastic bag in the garage for a season, but it does not have as nice a color the second year. Since I have a supply of new artemisia from the garden each year, I usually dismantle the tree by pulling out all the branches, which I keep in a plastic bag until the next year to use as bases for artemisia wreaths. The cone will last indefinitely.

Variation: if your home is too small for a real Christmas tree, you can make a fine substitute with a cone like this. Buy or beg from friends in the country a few good-sized branches or a bag of small clippings of green arborvitae, juniper, cedar, or yew. Presto, a small tree for an apartment table, and it costs practically nothing. A small potted tree of this size would be dreadfully expensive.

Sphagnum Moss Tree
Materials:
    Styrofoam or hardware mesh cone
    fresh or dried, unmilled sphagnum moss
    waterproof tray, pie pan, or low bowl
    twine or heavy thread
    sprigs of greenery

If possible, gather green sphagnum moss from a handy swamp before hard frost, stuff it in a plastic bag, and keep in a cold spot until needed. Lacking such a supply, you can buy dried sphagnum in small bales. Make sure that it has not been screened but is rather the unmilled whole moss. Put a generous supply (depending on how big the tree is to be) in a bucket of water, and let it soak overnight. Sphagnum is like a sponge, and this ability to absorb water is what makes it so useful.

After a thorough soaking, remove the moss, and wring out the excess water. Wrap the moss loosely around the frame (put the green side outward if it's fresh), then wind the string around the moss several times in a spiral from top to bottom, and tie a knot at the end. Make the layer of moss as thick as is practical. Place it on the tray, which should be wide enough to contain the whole frame.

I prefer the green moss, but since the base will be completely covered, it really makes no difference.

SPHAGNUM MOSS TREE

Plaster wet moss all over cone, and wrap string around loosely to hold in place

Shallow dish

Stick foliage into moss

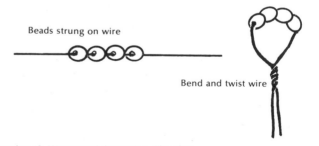

Beads strung on wire

Bend and twist wire

Drawing 10. Waterproof decoration. The glass beads are sold as Christmas tree ropes. The end of the wire can be inserted into the wet sphagnum at any point.

Fig. 3-6. Flat frame of hardware mesh for a tree
made of small clippings. The tree may be inserted
in a pot or hung on the wall.

Fig. 3-7. The frame half-covered to show how
clippings are inserted.

Once the base has been made, you can keep it for years. Let it dry completely, then store in a plastic bag. Remember to soak it overnight before using it again.

To decorate the base, stick small sprigs of greenery into the moss, beginning at the bottom. If your cone is short, use small-leaved evergreens like box, Japanese holly, yew, or juniper. On a frame as tall as 12 in. or more, English and American holly sprigs are quite in proportion. A few small berried twigs of winterberry (*Ilex verticillata*) add color, but if you have none, thread a few glass beads or tree balls on a piece of wire (as shown in Drawing 10), and stick them into the moss here and there. Any decorations for this tree must be waterproof.

This tree will stay lovely indoors for many weeks if you dampen the moss religiously. Pour water slowly at the top daily, and make sure that the bottom container always has some water in it. This is an ideal way to use pruning clippings, which are ideally made on many evergreens in late fall and early winter. Sometimes a few of them will even root!

Hardware Mesh Tree
Materials:
    flat tree form made from ¼-in. hardware mesh
    sprigs of greenery 6–12 in. long
Draw the tree in whatever size you want with a crayon on the mesh, and cut it out with wire cutters. Once made, this base can be used for many years. Choose greenery that lasts well, such as juniper, yew, arborvitae, or white pine.

Pick a perfectly straight sprig for the top, and weave its stem through the mesh several times so it stands upright. Now do the same on both sides and on the bottom. Sprigs 6 in. long are quite sufficient for a tree several feet tall. Smaller sprigs can be used near the top section. Work each outside sprig through two mesh holes to anchor it. Most of the other sprigs only have to be pushed through one hole, because they will rest on the lower ones. Continue to add sprigs from bottom to top until the whole frame is covered.

This tree can be hung on a wall or propped up against a stand. You can hang any size, but if you are

Fig. 3-8. Completed tree is trimmed with tiny red birds and white angels.

Fig. 3-9. Sprayed with gold paint, this juniper tree was still attractive (although very brittle) six months later.

going to prop it, keep it under 18 in.; otherwise the weight of the sprigs will bend it over, unless you back it with a strip of thin rigid metal or a piece of thin pipe wired vertically to the middle.

You can decorate this tree with almost anything, or you can leave it plain and simply tie a bright bow toward the bottom. It will stay in good shape for several weeks, especially if it is not placed near a direct heat source. Once I experimented with a tree made from juniper prunings, which was already a few weeks old and losing some of its color, by spraying it heavily with gold paint. Although it was very brittle, it still looked fine when I finally dismantled it many months later. This technique is very handy for people who run gift shops and need long-lasting display material. When you are finally through with the tree, discard the old branches, and store the frame for future use.

Variation: with the same frame, use small branches of dried materials such as artemisia, hydrangea, pampas plumes, or pearly everlasting.

Evening Primrose Tree
Materials:
    Styrofoam cone 6–12 in. tall
    many branches of evening primrose
        seed capsules
    white glue and dip pot
    clear glaze spray

Making this tree consists of nothing more than dipping the ends of the branches into the glue and sticking them into the cone. Start with a perfect piece for the top, measure two pieces for the bottom to establish the basic shape of the tree, then fill in until the cone is completely covered. Put larger clusters at the bottom, daintier ones on top. The tree will collect less dust if you give it a good coat of clear glaze spray when finished, but you can also spray it green, silver, or gold, or just tip the edges with color. Tiny decorations can be equally varied. One tree exhibited in our Christmas display at Bowman's Hill State Wildflower Preserve was dressed up with miniature birds. You can give your tree a fancy base, surround it with cut evergreen branches, or just let it sit by itself, balancing on its lower branches.

Fig. 3-10. Components of a white pine tree: two whole cones wired together and a cut-down cone for the top layers.

Fig. 3-11. Acorn cups and birthday candles decorate this white pine tree. The proportion is not perfect, however; the tree would look better if it were taller.

It is practically indestructible and it can be stored in a plastic bag for years of service. The cost is negligible, because evening primroses are roadside weeds everywhere. Be forewarned, however, that it takes a tremendous amount of them to make the tree full and pretty.

White Pine Cone Tree
Materials:
  holeless flower pot 6 in. high
  plaster of Paris
  sand or very dry dirt
  wooden dowel at least 18 in. long
  spool of wire (gauge 28)
  large supply of clean pine cones
  acorn cups

Any long, thinnish, open, true pine cone can be used for this tree, but those of the Eastern white pine are the best I know. Fresh cones with generous globs of white resin on their scale tips make the prettiest trees. If you can get a supply of them, add a bottle of fingernail polish remover to your supplies, spread newspaper on your work surface, and wear an apron or old clothes. You will have another indestructible tree when you finish, but you'll also have hands full of sticky resin. After using the polish remover to clean your hands, wash them well with soap. You can avoid much of the resinous mess if you bake your cones at 150°F. in the oven for 1–2 hours first. The resin melts into a shining mass, however, so line the pan with aluminum foil. Cones treated in this way are not quite as perky, perhaps, but they are a lot easier to work with, especially if you do this as a group project. They may also need a few shots of white floral spray at the end to relieve the uniform brown color, a step which is unnecessary with fresh cones.

If you don't have a flower pot without a hole, cut a piece of cardboard a little larger than the hole, and tape it securely in place inside the pot. Plastic pots are not as healthy for growing plants as clay ones, so this is a good way to use up an extra plastic one. Composition pots from old arrangements are also a possibility. The tree in Fig. 3-11 is in one of these. Whatever pot you choose, make sure it is sparklingly clean.

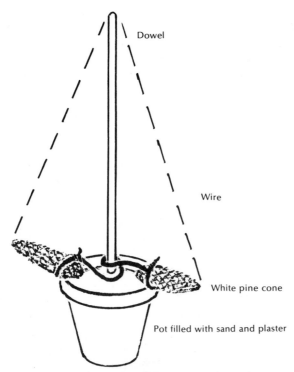

Dowel

Wire

White pine cone

Pot filled with sand and plaster

Drawing 11. Frame for making a white pine tree. A cone is fastened to each end of a piece of wire, which is then twisted once around the central dowel to prevent the tree from falling apart.

Fill the pot about two-thirds full with sand or very dry dirt. Mix about a cup of the plaster with just enough water to make it pliable: you need as thick a mixture as possible. Place dowel in center of pot, and push it down into the sand 3–4 in. Pour the wet plaster on top of the sand until it nearly reaches the top of the pot, smooth over, and prop the dowel so it stands straight. Let the mixture dry overnight. Plaster of Paris hardens quickly, so don't wet it until you are ready to use it. You could fill the whole pot with plaster, but you would need a lot, and it is heavy.

Grade your pine cones into three piles—the fattest and longest, the mediums, and the smallest. The first few layers of the tree require eight cones. Draw imaginary diagonal lines from the top of the dowel to the top of the pot, and decide how wide the tree should be at the bottom for the optimum effect of a graceful pyramid.

Cut a piece of wire about 4 in. longer than the distance from one side of the edge of the pyramid to the other. Now fasten two of the largest pine cones at either end of the wire by winding and twisting the wire securely around their fat stem end. Then wind the wire once around the dowel at approximately the midpoint of the wire. The two cones are then in place exactly opposite each other. Their wired ends should be slightly inside the outer rim of the pot for support.

Wire the next two cones in exactly the same manner, and place them on the dowel at right angles to the first pair. Put two more pairs of cones in the spaces between the first two, and the initial layer of the tree is complete. Sometimes the cones are so fat that you can fit only six cones per layer; don't worry, your tree will still be lovely.

When you start the second layer, the wire should be slightly shorter so that the shape of the tree conforms to the imaginary line toward the top. Each cone should lie between two cones of the layer underneath for the nicest shaping. You will eventually run out of cones small enough to continue the tapering. With your wire cutter begin to cut off some of the stem ends of the cones so that they become progressively shorter. As you approach the top, use only about 2 in. of cone and fewer cones per layer. At the very top, place one cone cut to the length needed to complete the desired height and proportion. Set its wired end on top of the last tier of cones, and work the wire down into the center of the tree. Use a daub of glue to make it secure.

This tree is very strong and will take a lot of punishment. It can be sprayed if desired, but I enjoy mine just as it is. If you want it very shiny, coat it with clear glaze. Trimming is again widely varied; I glue acorn cups here and there at the tips of the branches to hold very small, colored tree balls or candles. (Birthday-cake candles are the perfect size for this.) The tree is terribly inflammable, so you should never light any of them. If you melt the raw end of the candle to fasten it to the acorn cup, do this before you attach the latter to the tree. It is wiser to use tacky glue or a small glob of floral clay for this step, and either of these keeps the candles fresher-looking.

Pine Cone Favor Tree
Materials:
   small flower pot
   pyramidal-shaped pine cone
   plaster of Paris
   clear glaze spray

With this tree you can fashion a supply of table favors in a few minutes. Make sure that all cones are clean and dust-free and that the pots are equally

2

3

5

6

9

8

Color captions on page 2.

10

11

12

13

14

15

16

17

18

19

20

21

22

23

24

25

26

27

28

29

30

31

32

33

31

34

35

36

shining. Your only design problem is proportion. To look its best, the tree part should be at least twice as tall as the pot; three times is even better.

Block the hole in the bottom of the pot with a piece of tape, fill almost to the rim with wet, thick plaster, stick the stem of the pine cone into the plaster, and prop it in place until the plaster hardens. Decorate the tips of the cone with dried flowers, interesting seed pods, or tiny beads glued in place; then give the whole tree a coat of clear glaze. Glue a bright ribbon bow to the pot if desired.

You can make tiny bushes just as easily by sticking small sprigs of artemisia, pearly everlasting, or carefully dried goldenrod into the plaster while it is wet.

Variation: a topiary tree can be made almost as quickly. Proceed in the same way, but instead of using a pine cone for the tree, use a small tree twig that has at least two opposite branches. Trim these until you have stubs 1–2 in. long, depending on the height of the tree. Now glue pieces of the green-dyed reindeer lichen found in hobby shops to the twigs and the central leader until you have a ball of the size you wish. Make another smaller ball at the top. Or wire whole, perfect hydrangea balls to the twig.

Variation: with a thin dowel and two different-sized Styrofoam balls, you can make another kind of topiary tree in any size you want. Anchor the dowel in the pot as for the white pine tree. Push the larger ball down the dowel to about its mid-point, and glue it in place. (You may have to drill a hole in the ball first.) Glue the smaller ball to the top of the dowel. Once they are dry, glue small spruce or pine cones, sweetgum balls, or beech burrs all around both balls. Fill in any interstices with small cones and pods until no Styrofoam can be seen. Spray the balls with clear glaze, or gold or green floral spray. You can glue small strawflowers on them afterward if you wish.

Tree Plaques
Materials:
    plywood or Styrofoam tree form
    white glue and dip pot
    hanger
    assorted cones, pods, nuts, etc.
    findings from a sewing box

Only the availability of the materials limits the sort of two-dimensional tree you can make. A plywood base provides a sturdier hanging, which can be bigger and can use larger, heavier materials than a Styrofoam one. On the other hand, the Styrofoam base tends to have more depth, especially if a fairly thick piece is used. It is also easier to cut out with hand tools. A really splendiferous plaque is made by gluing a plywood backing to the Styrofoam tree.

The base can be made with a pot as part of the form (see Fig. 3-12) or simply as a tree with a big bow at the bottom to finish it off (see Fig. C-3). Both of these trees were made with an assortment of cones, pods, and nuts in much the same way as previously described for the heritage wreath. Note that the larger objects tend to be at the bottom of the tree and that certain striking items are repeated in a smaller size farther up. All interstices have been filled in, and the last step was a coat of clear glaze.

The tree in Fig. 3-13 is much easier. Only small Scotch pine cones were used; they were glued together as closely as possible to a Styrofoam base. The whole tree was sprayed with gold, and a ribbon was added to the pot, which was covered with green cloth. If you use Styrofoam to give depth, make sure that you glue some cones to the outer edges. If you use only plywood, make sure the decorative material is glued so that some of it extends over the outer edges. These techniques ensure a much more graceful effect than if the raw edges show and also make the outline a bit irregular, which I think is more interesting.

Another warning: attach the hanger to the back very securely before you do any decorating. Hardware stores have an assortment to choose from. Since the Styrofoam is soft, it is a good idea to anchor the hanger especially well. One way is to drill two small holes about 2 in. apart at a spot a few inches from the top. Using heavy taped wire, make a loop large enough to hang the plaque by, then tie a knot below the loop at the back and thread the two loose ends through the holes to the right side. Tie a square knot, leaving 1–2 in. of wire on both ends. Then glue these to the right side of the plaque. Glue your decorative material on top of the square knot and the

Fig. 3-12. Nut and cone tree plaque on a flat piece of plywood. Green velvet leaves were glued on the back as edging.

Fig. 3-13. A single type of small cone was used to cover the Styrofoam tree plaque. The entire tree got a coat of gold paint at the end.

ends to hide them and to add strength to the object.

Variation: even with a limited amount of dried cones or pods, you can make a very effective plaque. Cover the form with colored burlap, velvet, rough linen, or whatever, and glue this in place, extending it around to the back so the side edges are completely covered. Trim the edges with braid, rickrack, or small cones. One very effective plaque that I saw had heavy-rope glued to the edges. Attach what cones and pods you have to the tree surface in a vertical, horizontal, or spiral pattern, or even one to suggest branches. While this is not quite as effective as a completely covered form, it uses far less raw materials.

What I am trying to emphasize is that a two-dimensional tree can be put together in a wide variety of ways with an assortment of materials. The same techniques can be utilized to make almost any form imaginable: five or six-pointed stars, bells, birds, Easter rabbits, snowmen, angels, Santas—you name it.

Variation: cut a three-dimensional Styrofoam form such as a bell or cone exactly in half lengthwise with a serrated carving knife or coping saw. Then glue the flat side to a backing of some sort, either the same size and shape as the Styrofoam or a larger plaque behind it. When decorated, the form protrudes in a much more interesting manner than if it were simply a flat outline. One bell that I like was trimmed with overlapping scales from large pine cones and then given a good coat of clear glaze. The clapper was beaded with yellow popcorn, and a heavy yellow rope of braided yarn ran from the top in extending curves down either side of the plaque to end in irregular knots. The rope was also glued in place.

The bell could just as easily have been covered with sweet-gum balls or a combination of items. And it could have been sprayed white or silver and used for wedding parties instead of New Year's Eve. I saw a snowman once that had been made in the same way, with hemispheres of different sizes glued on their flat sides to a backing. It was hung on a door during the holiday season and had a bright red bow simulating the snowman's scarf. Only parts of the balls were decorated with cones, since the white of the Styrofoam was essential to the idea.

A Partridge in a Pear Tree

Materials:

    flower pot 6 in. high
    plaster of Paris
    sand
    interestingly shaped branch about 18 in. high

Here is another tree that need not be used just for one holiday. It is worth describing the kind of tree branch you need. It must have a straight bottom to go into the flower pot, but the top should branch. I think a tree with a horizontal branching habit such as dogwood or magnolia is the most interesting. Fruit trees with spurs are good too; you may even have a pear! In any case the branch should be relatively balanced, and it should have some twigs on at least two sides. Secure it in the pot as for the white pine tree.

Now hang some small pears in the tree. Unless you have access to Seckel pears, you'll probably have to settle for artificial ones. Three are usually enough for a small branch. You can either make or buy your partridge. It doesn't have to look much like a partridge, so long as it's definitely a bird, particularly if you have small children. Partridges have wide tails, so the easiest way to make it recognizable is to gild a martynia pod, stick a bunch of pretty feathers in the hole where the seeds come out, and add a few more for wings. Put it on the branch with a small daub of floral clay.

Variation: fasten the branch to a flat base by drilling a hole in the base and gluing the branch in it. Hide the glue with a few bits of moss or some dried flowers. I like the pot better, because it is easier to make and less likely to break off or tip over.

Variation: the same basic tree can be decorated with almost anything throughout the year. The partridge is easily detached from the floral clay. I suppose you could have a tree full of tiny birds if you wished. My friends often hang empty, colored eggs on their trees at Easter. Hearts or cherries in February, owls or tiny jack-o'-lanterns in November—these are just a few suggestions.

If you store it carefully between uses, the basic tree can last the lifetime of your children and your grandchildren too, for that matter.

Gumdrop Tree

Materials:

    flower pot 5–6 in. high
    plaster of Paris
    sand
    branch of hardy orange (*Poncirus trifoliata*)

You can just as rightly call this a birthday tree, a sugarplum tree, or whatever your children prefer. It is really a year-round decoration for the family with small people. Perhaps we can call it simply a fun tree.

For those of you who live in the far north, I wish I could offer a suitable substitute for the hardy orange. Barberry is not strong enough; roses and firethorn do not branch gracefully enough. Look for a piece of hardy orange if you come to warmer latitudes. It bears quantities of alarmingly stout, sharp thorns and is thickly branched. To be stuck in a thicket of it would be a nightmare, but it is ideal for our purpose.

You need a nicely branched symmetrical piece that is not much taller than 15 in. Trim it if necessary so it does not extend too far on one side, for the weight of the candy that you will be putting on it is considerable, and you don't want it to tip. As a further precaution, carefully clip off the thin tip of each thorn so there is no chance of its breaking off inside a piece of candy. The thorns are long enough without the tip. Wash the entire branch in soapy water, and rinse thoroughly. After every use, wash it again, and store in a clean plastic bag.

Secure the tree in a pot as with the white pine tree. If there is a small thorned branch near the bottom, try to stick part of that in the plaster for a good anchor. When you are ready to use the tree, attach gumdrops, marshmallows, or any other soft candies that do not run by sticking them on the thorns. For the tree in Fig. C-5, I used gumdrops of a single color and green spearmint leaves, but you can just as well use several colors. The spearmint leaves are very heavy; use them sparingly, or the tree will become top-heavy.

If your branch was cut from a live tree, it will stay green for a year or two, but eventually it browns. If this bothers you, color the branches with waterproof, lead-free paint. (Don't paint the thorns where you put the candy.) I have a friend who remembers a gumdrop tree from her childhood, and her mother had painted its branches white. It is a lot easier to make sure that a white tree is clean when you wash it after using. Marzipan fruits and flowers or even fancy, dried real fruits can also be served on the tree to jazz up a child's dinner.

Norfolk Island Pine (*Araucaria excelsa*)

I started this chapter with a bit of philosophy, and I shall end in a similar vein. All the foregoing projects have been substitutes for trees. Gay, clever, but nevertheless dead, whatever their origin. Especially if you live in an apartment, you may long for real trees. I would probably go around madly repeating a disgusting refrain from my own childhood, "Fir Yew I Pine and Balsam." If you linger near that brink, consider this last tree.

Reputedly the first Norfolk Island pines in this country came from their original Pacific homes on New England whaling ships. They make fine house trees. They do best with cool treatment (not much above 60°F. at night), but they grow nicely even in north window light. If you turn the pot 90° whenever you water the tree, the main trunk will remain straight. If your home is very dry, set the pot on a shallow tray filled to the top with pebbles, and keep water in the tray all winter.

Under house conditions you do not want the tree to grow too fast, so feed it only a few times a year with soluble house plant fertilizer. During the summer you can put it outside, but direct sun burns the foliage, so keep it shaded. Nowadays even supermarkets sell Norfolk Island pines as pot plants, and small ones are not very expensive for an investment that will last many years. Mine is now just 2 ft. tall and has been transplanted to a large clay pot 9 in. in top diameter where I hope it will stay happy for years.

The soft feathery branches grow in tiers, and a healthy tree has a soft, dark green color. Aside from the pleasure of having a living tree indoors, it offers exciting possibilities for holidays. When it was still small, I once decorated mine with tiny red birds and bows of thin, white, velvet ribbon, another time with tiny Christmas-tree balls. I can recommend it as a friendly companion all year round too.

4
green wreaths and swags

Fig. 4-1. In using Frame C (Drawing 4), each group of clippings should lie in the same direction to hide the stems of its predecessors. The bunch of juniper on the right was placed here only to show the comparative sizes of each layer.

Few holiday preparations bring the gardener more satisfaction than fashioning wreaths and swags from his own greenery. The custom of bringing greens into the house stretches back much further than recorded history. Today we may not think about assuaging evil spirits when we hang a bough indoors, but the action may benefit our psyches nevertheless. Too many of us are out of touch with the natural world, and the smell of balsam is a comforting reminder.

What type of green decoration you make depends somewhat on the amount of material available, but you do not need a lot. All but the smallest evergreen can give up a few sprigs, and most trees grow fuller with a little pruning. By doing this job in early winter when you need greens for decorations, you accomplish two things with one cut.

Broad-leaved evergreens like holly, rhododendron, pieris, osmanthus, leucothoe, cherry laurel,

and mountain laurel are actually ideally pruned then. Summer cutting is apt to stimulate new growth, which may not harden off sufficiently before cold weather comes; if too soft, such new twigs winterkill. Early spring pruning is often neglected in the press of other work.

Severe cold and frigid wind often mar the foliage of the broad-leaved evergreens, so it is wise not to delay if you live in a northern climate. I usually prune (near Philadelphia) on a nice day no later than the first week of December. I put large branches in buckets of water, and they keep beautifully in my cool laundry room until I need them. Small clippings are sprinkled lightly with water, packed in sealed plastic bags and kept under similar cool conditions until I start my wreaths. Needled evergreens can be cut closer to when you want them. Store them in water also, or at least in a cold place, if you aren't using them immediately.

Basically, the process consists of attaching your clippings to a frame. Outdoor wreaths likely to be subjected to wind and weather require stronger, more durable frames than those for indoor decoration. Most frames can be salvaged after the holidays. After the old greens are removed, they are easy to store. You will gradually accumulate a fine supply of frames, which will allow some leeway in the future.

Many florists sell some wire frames. Florist supply houses are an even better source. Since each type of frame is treated slightly differently, we will consider them separately, but the greens for each are essentially the same. If you look carefully at a commercially made green wreath, you'll see that it is not constructed only from tips. Instead, the smart nurseryman cuts larger branches into smaller lengths. The stub ends are used inside to make a bunch nice and full, and one perfect tip hides them on top where it shows. You should use the same technique.

You can make a fine wreath from clippings of a single species of evergreen if you have a large supply, or you can use several varieties. In the latter case, each bunch of clippings to be fastened around the frame should contain the same mixture of types for uniformity. Similarly, try to make each individual bunch the same size so your wreath will not bulge in one spot and look thin in another. Don't be afraid to mix needled and broad-leaved evergreens together.

For the smallest frames, use clippings no longer than 6 in. For frames over 14 in. in diameter, the clippings may range from 6–10 in. in length. When working with a type like white pine, which has spaces between its needle clusters, you may need at least ten clippings of various lengths for each bunch to make your wreath full enough. A more luxuriously needled type like Douglas fir needs only four or five clippings per bunch. Some other good ones to consider are juniper, balsam, spruce, arborvitae, yew, and cedar, as well as the rarer broad-leaved evergreens like holly.

A piece of wet Oasis, half a good-sized apple, or a flattish potato may be fastened with wire at an approximate spot on any indoor frame. Holes punched with a skewer will allow you to insert small clippings of greens to make a focal point. Without this extra moisture, broad-leaved evergreen clippings will not stand up very long in a warm house.

In the following descriptions of various wreaths, the letters refer to the frames pictured in Drawing 4.

Bent Wire Wreath

Materials:
    wire frame with side wires (Frame C)
    assorted short lengths of greenery
    ribbon

Use this frame to make the easiest, quickest wreaths. Start by gathering a cluster of clippings together, lay them all going the same way on the central frame, and bend the side wires over them to hold the greens in place. With this first cluster of clippings, gauge whether your bunch is thick enough to stay firmly in place under the wires. It must not be so bulky that the side wires won't bend over it, but the prunings must be thick enough to hold each other in tension under the wire (see Fig. 4-1). If necessary, use pliers to bend the side wires or wear heavy work gloves.

Now lay the next bunch of clippings over the first, placing the stems in the same direction to hide the raw bottoms of the first. Proceed in this manner until you come to the last bunch. Its raw stem ends should

Fig. 4-2. Completed juniper wreath on Frame C.

Figs. 4-3 and 4-4. Same wreath gives different effects according to its decorations. Bunches of white statice are much daintier than large gilt birds. The white ribbon has a gold design.

be tucked under the greens of the first cluster before you bend the last set of wires over it.

Until you have made a few evergreen wreaths, the joining place at the end may not quite satisfy you. No matter; just attach your ribbon or any other decoration to that section to hide any imperfection. I find it easiest to work with the wreath flat on a table or on the floor rather than up in the air. The floral picks discussed in the decorative section of this chapter are particularly adaptable to Frame C wreaths, but you can get quite different effects from various types of decorative material.

When the holiday is over, pull out the greens, and scatter them in the garden where you have planted hardy spring bulbs. The evergreen needles seem to discourage hungry rabbits. To save the frame, you can either gently unbend the side wires each year or stuff the bunches under them as they are.

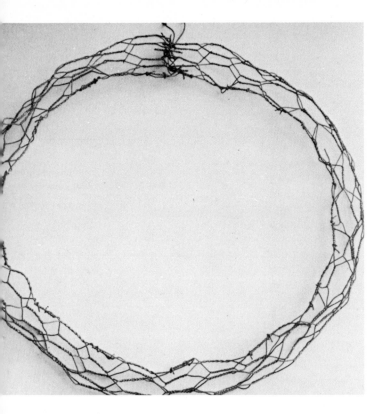

With a spool of wire, you can use the continuous wiring method already described in Chapter 2 (see Drawing 6). This goes much faster than wiring each bunch of greens separately. I always suggest continuous wiring for wreaths of dried material, because they are often used for several years, and it seems sensible to invest in a spool. A fresh wreath has a limited life, and the greens are easier to handle, so here you can use up odd pieces of wire. You can even do continuous wiring with heavy twine if you hold it very taut at all stages of the job.

Flat Wreath
Materials:
    double wire ring (Frame D)
    lengths of sturdy cloth 1½ in. wide
    safety pins
    assorted short lengths of greenery
    ribbon

An incredibly easy wreath can be made on Frame D without using any wire at all. Tear strips of fairly strong cloth about 1½ in. wide. Many craftsmen use dark green cloth. I prefer the strong sides of old sheets; once the greenery is in place, the cloth does not show anyway. Wind the strips flat around the frame, overlapping each preceding layer about 1 in. to form little pockets. Go all around the frame in one direction, and fasten the ends of the strips securely. Once wrapped, the frame can be used for years, so do a good job.

Making this wreath consists merely of pushing short stems of greens into each layer of pockets. It is ideal for white pine but adaptable to almost any green that is not too bulky. Each tier of greens overlaps its predecessor to hide the frame and the raw stems. This technique is highly recommended if you are limited to small clippings, because you do not need a lot of greenery.

Since it is quite flat, this wreath makes a good background for a decorative indoor wreath made on a Styrofoam base. For this purpose use an evergreen which endures heat without much needle drop; white pine, Douglas fir, and yew are the best.

Single Wire Wreath
Materials:
    wire coat hanger bent into a ring (Frame A)
      or
    crinkled wire ring (Frame B)
    floral tape
    assorted short lengths of greenery
    wire
    ribbon

A wooden or metal hoop, a tubular ring of chicken wire as illustrated in Fig. 4-5, or a frame made from willow withes as described in Chapter 2 can be used just as easily as the two frames suggested. In every case except that of the willow and the chicken-wire frames, wrap first with floral tape. This prevents the bunches of clippings from moving after they are wired in place.

There are two possible techniques. If you have many small pieces of wire handy, you can wire each bunch of clippings together first before attaching it to the frame. Wind the wire taut at least twice around the bottom of the stems so that they cannot work loose. Use a piece of wire long enough to fasten the bunch to the frame afterwards with it. Again, work in one direction to hide the stems of each cluster under the greens of the next.

Fig. 4-6. Small clippings of white pine are slipped into pockets of flat, wrapped Frame D in a few seconds. The sheet wrapping is several years old.

Fig. 4-7. Christmas mantel: the flat frame wreath of white pine is an excellent backing for the secondary wreath of gilded holly leaves glued into a Styrofoam ring.

Wicker Wreath

Materials:

    wicker or fiber frame
    assorted greenery
    ribbon

These frames come in many sizes and shapes. They are particularly good for indoor use, but I also use a big one on the outside of my picture window, which is subjected to very strong winds. I am afraid that a metal frame might break the glass, but the wicker one, secured with thin rope as in Fig. 4-8, has never caused any damage. I hang another wreath on the inside of the window to hide the back of the outside one.

Before adding the greens, you may work one or more rows of colored ribbon into the design. Then fasten the greens by weaving their stems between strands of wicker. Determine which side is to be the back, and put the raw ends there. For the simplest wreath, just insert greens all around the outside of the frame, overlapping each new layer to hide the bare part of the preceding clipping. One year I used very short holly clippings in this way most effectively (see Figs. 4-9 and 4-10). Cones can be wired on afterward.

A wicker circle frame allows even the most inexperienced to make quite elaborate-looking designs. It is the only way that I have ever successfully produced a crescent arrangement (see Fig. C-6).

If you have a wicker basket or any other holder, you can put a waterproof liner inside, cut a piece of Oasis, and display your greens indefinitely, as long as you keep adding water to the Oasis.

Swags

Materials:

    assorted lengths of evergreen branches
    medium-strength wire (gauge 26-28)
    assorted cones and pods
    ribbon

Greens don't have to be made into a wreath. If your evergreens can spare some branches instead of just clippings, you can fasten them together to make interesting decorations for doors and light posts. I have some junipers that are constantly outgrowing

Fig. 4-8. A wicker frame wreath is a safe choice for hanging against a big thermal window on the windy side of the house. Red ribbon suspends the wreath at the top; strong cord is run through the frame and secured on both sides to keep the wreath from blowing away.

Figs. 4-9 and 4-10. Holly prunings only 2–4 in. long are worked into a wicker frame to make this wreath; two large, berried holly branches are then added for color, and a red bow hides their raw stems and the wire fastening them to frame.

their quarters. Rather than moving the trees, I give them great haircuts every winter. By removing branches judiciously, you can practically hide the cuts on most evergreens. Some of these extra branches I use for swags; others I cut up into small sprigs, which supply the raw materials for many wreaths. While juniper holds up very well, it is quite scratchy. Use a pair of flexible work gloves.

I use three basic techniques to make swags. The easiest is to wire two nice full branches together in two places so that the foliage of each points in opposite directions. Then wire a few full smaller branchlets towards the center to hide the joining. The two sides can either be the same size, or one can be smaller than the other. The latter is suitable for fastening lengthwise to the top of a door, the shorter end up and the longer end extending down the door panel.

Figs. 4-11 and 4-12. Two ways to make a swag base. Top: this consists of two large branches wired together in opposite directions. The finished version is pictured in Fig. C-4. Bottom: this swag is made with three large branches wired together at the top.

Fig. 4-13. A few small sprays of white pine, some larch cones still on their twigs, and a red and white bow complete the three-branch swag.

Another design is slightly more difficult and requires three rather full branches at least 2 ft. long. The longest goes in the center, the other two on either side. Wire them together securely in several places at the top so that they will stay in place. Camouflage the tops of the branches with a bow.

Variation: even if your branches are only about 1 ft. long, you can still make a fairly large swag. Make a frame with a piece of firm, dense Styrofoam wrapped in wide tape, a block of wood, or even a small log. Wire or staple the smaller branches to this frame. By overlapping branches, you can make several small ones look like a much bigger one.

A cluster of cones and pods here and there and a bright ribbon are all that you need to dress these swags up for any occasion, but there are more suggestions for decorating at the end of this chapter.

This is a good place to mention the modern storm

Fig. 4-14. A large swag of juniper branches helps to hide an ugly storm door. Ornaments include gold martynia birds, sweet-gum balls, red satin balls, and bleached milkweed pods.

door; with the energy shortage, we will be seeing more and more of them. I have lived with two of the ugliest versions for most of my adult life. Granted that they cut the winter wind, save fuel, flood part of the house with welcome afternoon sunshine when the inside door is open, and allow cooling breezes to enter in summer through their screen inserts—they are still aesthetically horrible, and at no time does this bother me more than around the holidays. It took me years to discover how to attach a wreath or swag to an aluminum door, but it can be done.

A wreath can be hung by slipping a length of ribbon through its center and then fastening the two ends of the ribbon with the glass insert. Remove the screws that fasten in the glass, tilt the glass out from the top, hold the two ends of the ribbon in place as you push the glass back in, and replace the screws. Measure the length of ribbon needed to hang the wreath at the desired height before you start. If the wreath is quite heavy, put a knot in each end of the ribbon, and let the knots hang free on the inside of the glass; this should prevent the heavy wreath from pulling the ribbons out of the glass.

A swag requires a different kind of anchor. Measure the height of the upper glass insert. Buy a continuous length of 4-in.-wide cloth ribbon two times the height of the insert plus 4 in. Remove the glass insert, and slip the ribbon around it the long way. Pull the ribbon taut, overlapping it on the outside of the glass, and fasten it with two large safety pins. Replace the insert with the ribbon in place. Fasten the top and bottom of the swag to the ribbon with wires. If you pull both of these wires very taut so that the ribbon is actually pinched in at those two spots, the swag will not be able to slide down, and it will also hide the safety pins and the overlap.

Arch

Materials:
  wire coat hanger bent into an arch
  floral tape
  assorted lengths of greenery
  ribbon

If you're tired of the traditional wreath and swag, why not try an arch? The easiest way to make one is to bend a wire coat hanger into an arch-shaped form with the wires more or less parallel and about 2 in. apart from each other. Leave the hook on for hanging, and hide it with a big bow.

Before you bend the coat hanger, wrap it with floral tape so the branches you wire on will not slip. The arch in Figs. 4-15 and 4-16 was made with small branches of arborvitae. This evergreen holds up quite well after picking, and its graceful growth habit makes it ideal for an arch. You'll need branches about 1 ft. long for the body of the arch. Measure your branches against the arch until you have four of the same size. Wire one pair in two places to the top of the arch, the other to the bottom, both of them pointing towards the outer edge. Then fill in with smaller pieces of foliage until neither the wire nor the bare branches show. You can put a cluster of cones on either side.

You can bend your coat hanger just as easily into a straight line instead of an arch, and you can make the arch as full or as narrow as the space available for it requires. If you want a bigger arch than this, you can make a frame out of stout wire. I suppose that if you needed a really huge one, you would have to have it made out of pipe, because the bigger the arch, the

Figs. 4-15 and 4-16. A coat hanger bent into a semicircle makes a frame for an arch. The drop and the cones were wired on after the greenery was in place. A big ribbon bow hides the top of the drop.

Fig. 4-17. Cones can be wired on a floral pick ahead of time and used over and over.

Fig. 4-18. Floral pick slips into a wreath for quick decorating.

greater the weight of the branches wired to it. In this case it would be wise to wire a series of smaller branches, which weigh less than great boughs.

Decorating Your Greenery

A wreath of greens is beautiful by itself, but most of us want to add something to it. This is where making your own decorations becomes most fun. You may merely add a lovely bow in whatever shade goes with your color scheme. Or you may fasten a few cones, dried flowers, berried twigs, or bright ornaments. Most of these can be simply wired to the wreath or swag.

You can also use floral picks. They are quite inexpensive to buy, but you can also make your own. Fasten a piece of flexible wire to a wooden pick, then wire on a large cone or a cluster of several different shapes and sizes (see Fig. 4-17). It is very easy to insert this into a wreath, working the pick between clippings for a good hold.

My best advice for your decorating is: use whatever you have around. Your own are always most satisfying. If you hang your wreath or swag on a door, secure the decorations very firmly, and avoid anything apt to drop or fall apart easily.

Certain additions are particularly effective with greens. Berried twigs of winterberry or other hollies are traditional, but you can make do with other things. The red hips of the obnoxious *Rosa multiflora* hedge can be wired together in bunches and placed against any greens, and they even last fairly well in a warm house. Many other berried shrubs can be incorporated. Your choice ranges from the tropical pepper berries to the bayberry of northern mountains. White statice or artemisia sprays, small bunches of pearly everlasting, groups of honesty pods, teasel "flowers," and clean milkweed pods converted into flowers or gilded are some suggestions to contrast with the greens. Pine cones always look good.

The heritage wreath made from a Styrofoam circle is a wonderful adjunct to an indoor wreath, as is its stronger wired counterpart to an outdoor one. The inset wreath can be slightly smaller than the green one or exactly the same diameter. The greens will still show on either side. The wreath of evening primrose seed capsules is one of my favorites against a backing of greens.

Sometimes in trying to be clever we overlook the simplest forms of decoration, even though they are often the most effective. This was brought home to me on a Christmas visit to a friend. Instead of making elaborate wreaths and swags, she had put just the branches themselves in strategic places. Along her bookshelves, which stretch the length of a room, she had put short twigs of white pine and little angel statues. Few of the branches were more than 1 ft. long, but they were so artfully arranged that I did not even notice the joinings. Above the arch to the dining room was one large branch of white pine with a perky bow of white ribbon. The wall sconces for her electric lights each had a smaller branch of pine similarly beribboned. White pine is ideal for such trimming, because of its graceful growth habit and its ability to stand up well to heat. Be warned, however, that white pine does exude resin; don't use it against cloth. You can substitute arborvitae, juniper, Douglas fir, or yew for care-free indoor use, although none of these stands up as well as white pine.

Another quick reminder: all greenery can be used in water, and many kinds of evergreen will last for months in a vase. In the winter months they substitute for flower bouquets very nicely.

With no trees of their own, apartment dwellers, of course, are handicapped. Some greenery is available for sale. Try to get it from a nursery out in the country where it is likely to be fresh cut. If you buy a Christmas tree that's a little too big for your living room, cut off its lower branches and soak them in deep warm water overnight. These can be used for a swag or as part of a wreath.

Whatever kind of greenery you use and however you decorate it, you'll find that it lends a special touch to your holiday, because it will be a unique expression of yourself.

Fig. 4-19. Another way to dress up a wicker frame covered with holly prunings. White statice, bunches of red rose hips, and gilded sweet-gum balls are wired onto the frame after the holly is in place.

5
kissing balls, mobiles, and hangy downs

Fig. 5-1. Large open burrs of European beech were fitted as closely together as possible to cover this big kissing ball. Tiny starflowers and sprigs of white pearly everlasting add color.

Mobiles and other kinds of hangydowns have absolutely no serious purpose. That's what makes them so much fun. So let yourself go. Herewith a few suggestions to get you started.

Permanent Kissing Ball
Materials:
    Styrofoam ball at least 2 in. in diameter
    white glue and dip pot
    assorted pods, cones, etc.
    wooden matchstick
    heavy wire
    clear glaze spray
    thin ribbon

Choose a Styrofoam ball in a size that is appropriate for the spot where it will hang. For a spacious, high-ceilinged hall a sphere 5 in. in diameter is not too large, but for most modern homes a 2–3 in. sphere is a better choice. Keep in mind that the finished kissing ball will measure at least 2 in. more in diameter, since the cones and pods protrude from its surface.

Measure a piece of heavy wire (gauge 24 is strong enough) at least 3 in. longer than the diameter of your sphere, and poke it through from North Pole to South Pole. At one end, wind the wire twice around a piece of wooden matchstick or a small twig. This anchors it so it won't pull through the Styrofoam. Pull the wire taut, and at the other end make a loop to hang the ball easily later.

Decorating consists of gluing items to the sphere as closely together as possible. What you use depends on what you have available. You could use large beech burrs (as in Fig. 5-1), sweet-gum balls, or small Scotch pine cones. If your raw material has some sort of stem, as do many pods, simply dip the stem in glue, and stick it into the sphere. Stemless items stay better if you make an indentation first with your finger in the soft Styrofoam.

The most interesting kissing balls I've made used a combination of small Scotch pine cones, althea pods, beech burrs, small spruce cones, and sweet-gum balls. They were placed so that two of the same item were never together. The interstices were filled with small sprigs of pearly everlasting, also glued in place. You can use almost any dried flower.

To finish, spray with several light coats of clear glaze, unless you plan to gild the ball. The latter treatment is quite lovely with sweet-gum balls or peach pits, as in the variation below, but it spoils the interplay of the soft natural colors of mixed cones and pods. Spray lightly if you gild to prevent the paint from dripping onto the Styrofoam and eating it up.

I usually tie a small piece of bright ribbon at the top to hide the twist below the loop in the wire. At the bottom, you can fasten a piece of fresh mistletoe or some greens with a straight hairpin stuck into the sphere between the cones. Or you can make a pretty bow with streamers from thin ribbon as explained in Drawing 1, and fasten it with a corsage pin.

To store these kissing balls, remove the ribbon and any live material, and tie up in a plastic bag with a few mothballs.

Variation: instead of gluing dried flowers between the interstices of the cones and pods, stick tiny fresh sprigs of a small-leaved evergreen such as box, Japanese holly, or yew in the openings, and trim with a bow and streamers.

Variation: trim the Styrofoam sphere entirely with peach pits. Make an indentation in the Styrofoam with the pit first, then dip it in glue, and insert it. Do a small section at one sitting, prop the ball until the glue hardens, then do some more. When all the pits are firmly in place, gild the entire ball, and trim with greens or a ribbon on the bottom.

Hoop Kissing Ball
Materials:
    two embroidery hoops
      or
    two small willow hoops
    wire or thread
    tacky white glue and dip pot
    small cones and pods
    thin ribbon (optional)
    artificial bird (optional)

Embroidery hoops are available in needlework shops, but if you cannot obtain them, you can make your own in any diameter by weaving some willow wands, as described in Chapter 1. You can wrap the hoops in bright ribbon; this is mandatory for a good gluing surface on hoops made of metal or woven material. Put one hoop inside the other, and fasten with wire or thread so they are at right angles to each other. At the top, make a hanger with a loop of wire.

Halves of sweet-gum balls work very well for decorating this kissing ball, but again, you can just as easily use an assortment of things, as long as they have a flattish surface so they can be glued to the hoop. Spray with glaze or gild, as with the previous balls. A bow of thin ribbon and streamers can be wired on at the bottom for a nice finishing touch. If your hoop has a metal slider, make sure to put it at the bottom or top so you can hide it with ribbon.

The bird fastened inside is optional but rather fun. Buy one in the right size, or make one according to the directions in Chapter 8. It can hang inside from the top of the hoop or be fastened with some floral clay to the bottom. One charming conceit is to suspend a small stained-glass bird or butterfly within the hoops. It moves with the air currents and sheds a lovely note when light strikes it.

Variation: using the continuous wiring method described in Chapter 2, fasten short sprigs of box or other small-leaved or small-needled greenery all around both hoops after they are secured together. This is particularly suitable for a cool room. Decorate with ribbons, berries, or a bright bird. Remove any fresh material before storing.

Live Kissing Ball
Materials:
    sphagnum moss
    strong thread
    wire hanger
    sprigs of holly, ivy, etc.
Either live green sphagnum moss or the unmilled dried kind can be used for this version of the kissing ball. If you have access to live moss, wrap it with the green side out; if you are using dried moss, soak a quantity overnight in a bucket of water.

To make the base, take enough moss to mold a ball a little bigger than a baseball but a bit smaller than a regulation softball. Squeeze it until it no longer drips, and wrap it around tightly about eight times from

KISSING BALL

North Pole to South Pole with the thread. I use the thread that is sold for strong button fastening. Change the direction of the thread as you wrap to make circles about 1 in. apart all around the sphere. This keeps the moss from raveling or falling apart. Fasten a piece of wire through the threads at the top as a hanger.

Now insert the sprigs of greenery. Pieces 2–5 in. long are quite big enough. I use one of my English holly hybrids for this, because its leaves are smaller than American holly. I cut the bulk of the sprigs from the male bush, then use up to a dozen berried ones from the female for decoration.

You can also use prunings from almost any other green of which you have a good supply, but holly, ivy, or box are nicest. Stick the sprigs about 1 in. into the sphagnum as closely together as needed to hide the moss base. Use a skewer if necessary to make the holes. If you have only a few bright berries, save those pieces until last, and place them on the lower half of the sphere where they will be most noticeable when you hang it.

Lacking any berry supply, you can decorate your ball very handily with small glass beads from the Christmas ornament box. Thread a few on a piece of wire about 5 in. long, cross the wire below the beads,

summer party with small stems of flowers among ivy or other greens.

When you have finished using your sphagnum ball, remove all live material and hang it up in an out-of-the-way spot to dry completely. Then store in a plastic bag. Merely let it soak overnight the next year, and it is ready to decorate again.

Variation: for a few days' use only you can utilize a citrus fruit, large apple, potato, osage orange, or a ball of wet Oasis in the same fashion. Make a sling of twine to hold it, and fasten at the top with a piece of wire for the hanger. Using a skewer if necessary to make holes first, stick the sprigs of greenery into the fruit as closely as needed to hide it. The moisture inside the fruit nurtures the greens for a little while. The Oasis base can be immersed to renew the water, but it is not as sturdy as the sphagnum ball.

Drops

Materials:
    woven rope 6–12 in. long
    thin wire
    assorted cones, nuts, and pods
    ribbon (optional)

I have tried to make the directions for the drop as clear as possible, but this is not an easy decoration to make. By all means, start with a small one, no longer than 6 in. It is much simpler to get the hang of it on a small scale; you can always advance to more elaborate efforts.

Use rope that has at least two strands. An old clothesline is ideal, but hemp rope can be utilized too. If all else fails, braid some heavy twine together. Tie a simple knot at either end to guard against fraying.

To make a drop that will lie flat against a wall or door (by far the easiest), put the rope on a table and work your design there. A drop that will be suspended in the air, however, must look good from every direction. I do that type by fastening the rope base to a dowel and suspending it from two chair backs, while I sit on the floor and swear a lot. The problem is that a free-hanging drop will not stay at one angle, and it twists constantly as you try to fill it in. Done well, however, it can be most effective.

and stick the two raw ends into the sphagnum ball (see Drawing 10). Do not use anything which is not waterproof. You can tie a small bright ribbon at the top to hide the wire hanger, but don't put cloth ribbon at the bottom; moisture will spoil it.

Sphagnum moss is like a sponge; it holds a tremendous amount of moisture. Greens like holly will not stay fresh in a heated house unless they are kept in water, but the sphagnum acts just as if it were a filled vase. Occasionally, however, this ball must be immersed in a pail of water for a short time to renew its moisture. Let it drip a little while afterwards in the sink to protect your floor. Treated in this way, a holly ball will stay fresh for many days. Even if you do not renew the water, the sphagnum will protect the holly for a few days, but you must remember that anything hanging dries out very quickly, because the hot air in a room rises to the ceiling. Outside on a porch this ball needs no renewal and may stay fresh for months during winter weather, especially if there is moisture in the air. The sunlight streaming on the holly ball in Fig. C-9 does not really show how gay the green and red looks in the dining-room arch where it normally hangs. I go to extra trouble to keep mine fresh for as long as possible, just because I love it. I've often wondered if I couldn't make a similar decoration for a

Drawing 13. The backbone of the drop is a piece of rope with at least two strands so that the wire of each cone can be inserted to stay in place. Knots at top and bottom keep the rope from raveling.

Fig. 5-3. Long drop utilizes magnolia leaves to give some width at the bottom. Greenery and ribbon would be added at the top if it were on display.

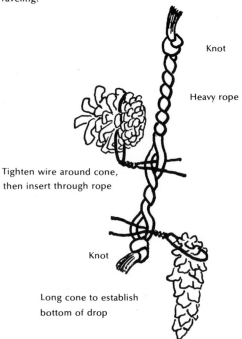

Knot

Heavy rope

Tighten wire around cone, then insert through rope

Knot

Long cone to establish bottom of drop

Whichever way you work, the first step is to find a really perfect cone or pod which comes to a point. I often use an immature white pine cone. Secure a piece of wire about 5–6 in. long to the top of this cone, then run one of its ends through the rope just above the bottom knot. The size of this cone establishes the ultimate length of your drop. I've seen a small bell used for the same purpose. To look its most graceful, the finished drop should first taper outward for a few inches as it advances towards the top, then curve slowly inward towards the rope at the top end. Work from bottom to top to make the backbone of the drop, then fill in as needed to complete the design.

For the flat drop, you can more or less arrange the pieces in a pattern on the table first. Use the same technique for the main structure of the three-dimensional drop too; fasten a piece of wire firmly around the middle of each cone, then secure it to the rope. Adjust the amount of wire according to where the cone is to hang. Big cones go toward the center, smaller ones nearer the outer edges or in spaces left between bigger items. Sometimes you can fasten one cone to one end of a wire, work the wire through the rope, and then put another cone on its other end. All this is easier said than done, but it is all possible. As you can see in Drawing 13, each cone must be fastened securely with a twist of wire around its middle before you work the wire through a strand of rope and twist it again to hold in place.

Eventually the pods and cones will hide the rope and the wires, especially if you fasten some close to the rope itself. Confine yourself to raw materials which are relatively sturdy, since the drop will get some wear and tear, although you can see in Fig. 5-3 that I used two dried magnolia leaves in my long one to add width. A varied assortment of cones is better than a single kind, but try to use more than one of most items to prevent too spotty an effect. If you can, use different sizes of the same kind of cone to hold the design together.

You might think that since the drop is to hang, it would be best to fasten the wire to one end of a cone, but it doesn't work that way; most are best wired near their centers so they can't flop around too much.

Fig. 5-4. Empty English walnut shells go to work. Left: ornament lined with aluminum foil. Center: basket edged with gold braid and filled with dried flowers. Right: ornament edged with strung gold sequins glued in place.

Nuts are very ornamental in a drop, but you will have to drill a hole through them for a wire. You can wrap the nuts in old nylon stockings, which are tightly stretched over the shell and then fastened at one end with a wire, but they are just not as pretty.

A one-sided drop can be hung on a wall with a ribbon on top to hide the knot or added to a swag of greens on a door. It is particularly adaptable to an arch of greenery (see Figs. 4-15 and 4-16).

If you make two quite similar flat drops, you can use them as practically indestructible table decorations. Put whatever you wish in the center of the table, then place the drops on either side of it, and fill in with a few evergreen sprigs. With such a ready-made accessory, you can arrive at a meeting and provide a quite splendid centerpiece in a few moments.

When you graduate to the three-dimensional drop, you will find that you must turn it constantly while you are working on it to make sure that it is full enough all around. Again, the size of the finished drop should be governed by where it is to hang. You could make a huge drop with sugar pine cones and other very large items, but unless you have the space to hang it, the whole thing will look ungainly. Don't make a drop much longer than 6 in. with small cones, or the proportions will be wrong.

English Walnut Ornaments
Materials:
    empty English walnut halves
    white glue
    findings of every sort
    thin wire, clear nylon thread, or
      fine fishing line

With a little help, your children can have lots of fun doing this. The end results can be used to ornament Christmas trees, mobiles, packages, dollhouses, and what-have-you.

Break the walnuts carefully so that you get some perfect shell halves. With a needle-nosed pliers, clean out all the inside membranes. Then, using a hand drill, or an awl, or the small blade of a jackknife, work gently until you have a tiny hole at one end of the shell; don't try to do this too close to the edge.

(For a basket, you'll have to drill a hole at either end.) Thread the wire through this hole for a hanger or handle. You can use fancy string or very thin ribbon as well as wire or thread. The golden mesh from a wine bottle made a fine hanger for many of my walnuts.

From now on, it's every taste to its own. You can paint or gild the outside of the shell or leave it *au naturel*. Little fingers have no trouble working aluminum or colored foil wrapping into the walnut; put a daub of glue in first to hold it. Then trim this carefully around the outer edge of the shell to make a background for whatever else strikes your fancy. (You can ignore this step if you wish and leave the inside plain.)

Inside you can make a tiny scene with some miniature figures or a tiny twig of evergreen sprayed green and decorated like a Christmas tree. A small cap from a tube or a baby seashell can be filled with tiny dried starflowers to look like a vase. You can trim the outside rim of the shell first with lace, thin rickrack, or gold braid. If you're making tiny baskets, you can glue a pea-sized scrap of Oasis in the walnut, then insert whatever small sprigs of dried materials you have with some glue to hold them in place. The three walnuts illustrated in Fig. 5-4 show some of these

Fig. 5-5. A Douglas fir cone forms the body of the smaller angel with flowing locks of milkweed silk; her wings are in a resting position.

Fig. 5-6. This gilded angel made from a large pine cone can sit as well as fly; her horn is a golf tee.

ideas. You can even make a tiny doll cradle with half a walnut shell and some odd pieces for a base or head shield and tuck a miniature doll inside with a scrap for a blanket.

Variation: if you're a wastrel, you could cover whole walnuts with a circle of foil a bit larger than the nut and fasten a wire to the top end where you've crumpled the foil together. Much more thriftily, put two halves of an empty nut back together with a drop of glue, and then wrap. Since foil now comes in every shade, these can be very colorful ornaments either to hang or to place in a holiday arrangement.

Flying Angels
Materials:
    pine cones
    milkweed pods
    tacky white glue and dip pot
    acorns and empty cups
    thin wire

Like birds, angels were meant to fly, so they make a perfect hangydown. Depending on the size of the cones available, they can be used as single decorations suspended from a beam, or bough, or a light fixture, or they can be made in quantity to decorate the Christmas tree. They also make perfect objects for a holiday mobile.

Try your hand first at larger angels made from clean white pine or Norway spruce cones. Those that measure 4–5 in. long fit the usual size of field milkweed pods perfectly. For really diminutive angels, use smaller cones, and cut milkweed wings to fit. Even when very dry, milkweed pods can be trimmed carefully with sharp shears. Check Chapter 1 for how to gather and dry the pods, for your angels should have the cleanest, best ones. Choose the acorns and cups for the heads and halos in proportion to the size of the bodies. There are many kinds of oaks, and the size and shape of their acorns vary widely.

The general directions are the same for all sizes of angels. Wind a piece of thin wire tightly around the cone near the top with the ends coming out at what will be the back of the angel; this is the hanger. If the cone is not perfectly straight, it seems to look more graceful in flight if the inside of the curve is to the back.

90

Glue an acorn cup backwards to the top of an acorn to make a halo, and gild it if desired. When this is dry, glue the acorn to the stem end of the cone. You may paint features on the face if you wish; eyes, eyebrows, and a mouth are quite sufficient, since the bump on the acorn is a ready-made nose.

If you gathered the milkweed pods early, they will have dried to a soft green on the outside and a light, shiny, cream color on the inside. These pods are decorative in themselves, but you may gild them if you wish. Old pods require the gold paint to hide their drabness.

Try to find two milkweed pods which match in shape. If you are using a smaller cone, you can split one pod in half to make a pair of wings. A somewhat passive angel is made by gluing the wings close to the body and pointing downward, as in Fig. 5-5. I prefer my angels in a flying position with the wings pointing upward or outward. If I am leaving the pods natural, I put the shiny side to the front, but you can just as well glue them to the back of the cone the other way so they appear to be streaming behind the body. The rough, green outer surface of the pods takes gold paint beautifully, incidentally.

One good way to fasten the wings is to dip the fatter edge of the pod in the glue and work it under one of the cone scales near the top; repeat on the other side, trying to get both wings in a similar flight position. You may have to prop them in place until the glue sets, even if you are using tacky vintage glue.

You may want to give your angels pipe-cleaner arms or other adornment. Milkweed silk makes great angel hair. You can also spray the whole article gold, silver, or white after it is finished. The angel in Fig. 5-6 is almost too big to hang except in a very large space. Her body was made with a large, round cone that sits very well, so she can be perched on a bough of the Christmas tree or with some greens as part of a display on a flat surface. If you intend to use an angel that way, don't bother to attach a hanging wire.

Variation: if you have a supply of fluffy white duck or goose feathers, you can make some sweet angels with small spruce cones for the bodies, acorn heads in proportion, and a feather glued into each side of the cones for wings. If you have bigger feathers, try the same idea with larger cones, but use just the top few inches of the plume, cutting it off at a point in proportion to the body.

Mobiles

Materials:
    wood or metal for arms
        or
    wicker or Styrofoam ring
    white glue and floral clay
    twine, wire, or ribbon, as indicated
    clear nylon thread or thin fishing line
    hangydowns

The mobile is a relatively recent form of decoration in comparison with the ancient lineage of the wreath. My dictionary defines it as: a piece of sculpture that has delicately balanced units constructed of rods and sheets of metal or other material and is suspended in mid-air by wire or twine so that the individual parts can move independently, as when stirred by a breeze.

This is an elaborate description of what is essentially a very simple art form. The joker is that phrase "delicately balanced." You can buy mobiles with many arms and intricate balance; if you'd like to make your own, start simply and work up. You attain the balance by playing with the weights of the hangydown item, the lengths of the lines on which they are suspended, and their placement along a crossbar in relation to the other things also hanging from the bar.

It is also important to attach the line supporting an individual item for a mobile to the item at its point of balance. This is easy to determine on a walnut basket, but the long-tailed peacocks in Fig. 5-7 were absolute demons, and I finally gave up trying to balance them perfectly. Nylon thread is terribly hard to handle, but it is strong and less visible than twine. When you hang your mobile, give it a spot out of reach of small children and tall heads, and just enjoy it. Even in a still room, it will seldom remain motionless, as I found when I tried to take the photograph for this book.

The easiest mobile starts with a single horizontal bar of some sort. It can be a straight length of metal or wood, a twisted piece of metal, an oddly contorted

Fig. 5-7. Assorted birds on this mobile refused to stay still even for their picture.

Drawing 14. Christmas mobile shows one way to avoid too much symmetry, but balancing is much harder with this type.

branch, or a piece of driftwood. A metal arm can be bent slightly so it arches. In any case, determine the mid-point of the arm by trial balances on a finger, then glue a length of string as a hanger at that point. You can experiment with the balances by using a small glob of floral clay to hold the line temporarily until you're satisfied. Then cover it with glue for a good bond. Suspend the bar so it hangs free.

Now attach at least four hangydowns on lines as long as necessary to look in proportion to the horizontal bar. Put the items on in pairs. Tie on the first of a pair where you want it, then move its mate back and forth until you find the exact spot on the bar where the two balance. Glue these two in place. Repeat with another pair. The clear nylon thread or fishing line is the least obtrusive when you look at the mobile, but you can also use ribbon and consider the line as part of the pattern.

A more elaborate mobile with three or four arms can be made just as easily; the arms can be of either the same or different lengths. Fasten them together with a single cotter pin through the exact middle of each arm. You can make the cotter pin from a piece of strong wire. Fan the arms out symmetrically, and weave some decorative twine around the middle so the arms remain separated. You will suspend this

mobile from the ceiling with a line through the loop of the cotter pin. Each arm will have a hangydown on either end; vary the lengths of the line from arm to arm, balancing by pairs again. Your problems of balance will be far less if the two hangydowns for each arm are similar in shape and weight.

Another mobile for beginners is made with a round woven wicker ring. Fasten a piece of wire through its center to suspend it, and tie the hangydowns on lines of varying lengths by pairs opposite each other around the outside of the ring. Balance one pair before attaching another set.

If you use a plain Styrofoam ring (or a similar shape in any other kind of material), wrap it tightly with ribbon first to make it a bit more decorative. You will have to make at least four crossbars to hang it with. One way is to tie lengths of ribbon at the four quarters of the ring, bring the lengths of ribbon together in the center, and knot. The ring will then hang from the ceiling at that point. The hangydowns are then attached as with the wicker ring.

Do you think you are ready to make more complicated things? Start with one long main arm. From either or both of its ends you can hang a smaller crossbar. Before you do that, however, balance each of the smaller crossbars separately with their hangy-

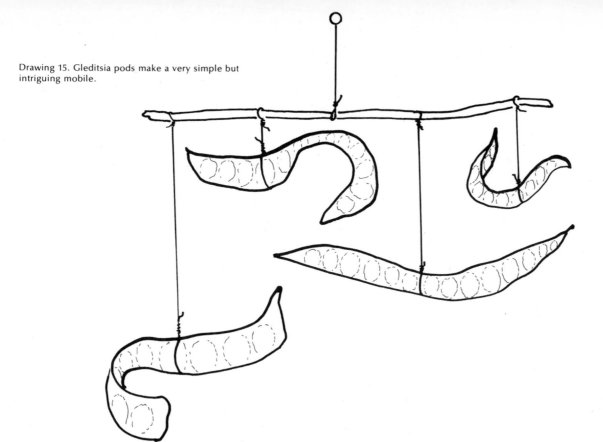

Drawing 15. Gleditsia pods make a very simple but intriguing mobile.

downs glued in place. You can continue making subcrossbars with their own crossbars indefinitely. Balsa wood ¼–½ in. square is one possibility for the bars. Light coat hangers can be cut for bars too, but file the ends or wrap them with floral tape so they aren't dangerously sharp. The diameter of the wood or metal is determined by how long the bars are to be and how heavy an object they must support. You could work up to lengths of pipe for that matter, but lighter arms and hangydowns react best to air currents. You miss out on the charm of a mobile if it remains motionless.

Somewhere along the line obviously, you'll have to decide what kind of hangydowns to have on your mobile. Their weight and size, after all, determines what you need for the arms. Nature, with an assist from you, offers an infinite number of possibilities.

One of the most unusual mobiles in my experience hangs in a college dormitory. Three wire coat hangers form its structural base. The hanger end of the top one is squeezed together, and a piece of fishing line through that loop attaches to a hook in the ceiling. With their hanger hooks similarly squeezed, the other two are suspended at either end of the first. Floating from all of them on various lengths of fishing line is the craziest collection of honey locust pods. When an air current starts them cavorting, it is like seeing a group of snakes weaving around in mid-air. Some hang from holes punched in the end of the pod, others from holes midway down the pod. Most honey locust pods are only slightly curved. This was a rare collection of weirdly bent S's, C's, E's, and every form in between. Each pod had been polished with furniture oil to make it shine; a shot of clear glaze spray would make dusting easier. The effect of even a few of these pods in a mobile is suggested by Drawing 15. Imagine them in a breeze.

Not everyone goes for a mobile this strange. Birds are a natural. Try the kinds described in Chapter 8. You could glue a loop of wire to one of the owls in the same chapter or use a pair of dried butterflies. The walnut halves and angels mentioned earlier in this chapter could be used too, as could the pixies in Chapter 8. You can even make tiny plaques with scenes. Small Styrofoam balls covered with pods and cones, strawflowers, or just interesting pine cones or seashells can be utilized. Or try any combination thereof, but use them in pairs of fairly similar things to make the balancing easier. The sky, or at least the ceiling, is your only limit.

6
candle
and
mantel
decor-
ations

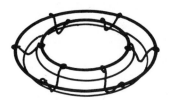

Frame E

Greenery

Sphagnum moss
packed into frame

Candles

Waterproof tray

Drawing 16. Trough frame filled with wet
sphagnum in which evergreen sprigs are inserted
makes a fireproof setting for candles.

Even with unlimited electricity and heat, mankind still loves candles and fireplaces. Perhaps it is some atavistic urge in all of us, dating back to the days when fire was our only source of both heat and light after the sun went down.

As much as we love to play with fire, I cannot start this chapter without first warning you that almost any dried material is highly inflammable. Never let a candle burn too low in such a holder, and never leave it unattended or within the reach of small children, strong wind currents, or unruly pets.

As every woman knows, candlelight is very kind to a face in which age has begun to etch a few lines here and there. The simplest meal gains an unhurried graciousness when served by candlelight or at least with lighted tapers on the table. So don't limit your use of them just to holidays or dinner parties. You can make decorations from natural materials that are useful most of the year. With this philosophy, changing the candle from red to pink doesn't mean "Christmas is over" so much as "Spring is coming."

Sphagnum Moss Candle Ring
Materials:
  waterproof tray
  round trough ring
  supply of wet sphagnum moss, fresh
    or dried
  fresh evergreen prunings
  assorted candles

Round trough rings in several sizes are usually available at florist supply shops. They are widely used for cemetery work, because they are very strong. If you cannot obtain one, you can make a fair substitute by cutting a length of chicken wire 4–5 in. wide and long enough to make a ring to fit your tray. (You can determine this by measuring the outer edge of the tray with a piece of string to get the circumference.) Starting with a long strip of flat chicken wire, bend it to form a trough, curve it into a ring, and fasten the two raw ends together. Take time to bend down all the cut edges of wire on the sides of the trough, for it can be a companion for many years, and you might as well make the relationship a bloodless one. This is somewhat similar to the chicken wire wreath frame in

Fig. 6-1. Paulownia pod halves were used to make
the strong circular design on this candle ring, and
other materials are also repeated regulariy.

Fig. 4-5, but the trough is open on top so you can stuff the moss in easily. (For the wreath frame, you make a complete thin tube so you can tie the wire around it.)

Don't use a silver tray under this decoration; it would get very tarnished by the wet wires. You can approximate the same effect by covering a large plate or pie pan with aluminum foil tucked well underneath to hide its torn edges. If you cannot obtain fresh sphagnum, you may find it easier and neater to line the trough with foil too before you stuff the wet moss into it.

All you do now is pack the trough with wet sphagnum and insert the pruning sprigs into it. Almost anything can be used for this purpose, but some of the prettiest winter greens include ivy, holly, osmanthus, pieris, leucothoe, and magnolia. During other seasons you can even put flowers from the garden in the ring, as long as the moss is kept wet. Add a few greens to hide the moss. Don't be surprised if some plants like ivy put forth roots.

Inside the ring you can put one very big candle or a combination of three candles of different heights, thicknesses, and even colors, for that matter. Stick them solidly to the tray with wax or floral clay so they won't topple. One advantage of this tray, aside from its aesthetic characteristics, is that it is fairly fireproof. You could use it for a children's party or for a buffet where people will be going in and out a lot without worrying.

You can also use this tray and decorated ring to display a statue, a pile of Christmas ornaments, or even fruit. As long as you remember to add water daily to the moss, the greens in it will remain in nice condition for literally weeks.

Candle Ring
Materials:
Styrofoam ring 5½–6 in. in diameter
  ½–1 in. thick
floral tape
white glue and dip pot
assorted cones, nuts, pods, etc.
clear glaze spray
felt (optional)
Of all the craft projects in this book, this is my personal favorite. Over the past few years my compatriots in the Doylestown Nature Club have made hundreds of them. The demand never seems to slacken. What is even more surprising is that a nucleus of no more than ten women, using the same basic ingredients, can turn out so many different versions.

On one occasion I was asked to match a candle ring sitting right in front of me, and the duplicate was only a fair copy. This is both the fault and the virtue of nature itself. A machine can turn out a million plastic parts, each as identical to its predecessor as to its successor, but peas in a pod are not all alike. You can gather dozens of horse-chestnuts from the same tree without finding two that match exactly. Moreover, you yourself are not the same person from day to day, and your own imagination shifts your emphasis continually. My pictures will show you some basic patterns; by all means, strike off on your own. Certain techniques will make your task a bit easier.

The Styrofoam ring described in the recipe is the most useful size. If you cannot buy it, cut it out of a sheet of Styrofoam with a serrated knife. The diameter of the hole should be about 3½ in. This allows you to use a candle 2–3 in. in diameter and still have a little leeway in case a few of the decorations project into the hole. Styrofoam ½ in. thick is preferable.

Wrap the ring all the way around with overlapping layers of floral tape to strengthen it. The first step in decorating is to cover the outer edge of the ring in the same way as with the heritage wreaths in Chapter 2. Do not trim the inner edge, however; you do not want anything to scratch the candle or make it hard to fit into the hole.

I have found that it is much easier to trim the outer edge with a single item. Make it a fairly sturdy one, since there is some wear probable at that point. Hemlock cones, tiny spruce cones, beech burrs, or small sweet-gum balls are very good choices. Glue them on as closely together as possible, using the dip pot and pins if necessary, as described for the heritage wreath. Allow to dry well, and remove any pins before going on to the next step.

The flat surface of the candle ring is only about 1 in. wide, but you have great latitude in what you can do in that space. The most attractive candle rings are

Fig. 6-2. Side view of the candle ring in Fig. 6-1 showing how tightly the items are fitted together to fill every crack.

Figs. 6-3 and 6-4. Foundations of two candle rings. Left: this consists of the same kind of cone alternating top and bottom. Right: this ring alternates peach pits and pods of swamp magnolia. Many small additional items will be glued in to fill the interstices before these rings are finished.

Figs. 6-5 and 6-6. Top: the candle ring started with concentric circles of hemlock, spruce, and Douglas fir cones. Bottom: when the interstices are completely filled, the foundation pattern is hardly discernible.

those which are not too flat, and the easiest way to prevent this is to glue some larger items on first. Horse-chestnuts, walnut halves, Scotch pine cones, or anything about 1 in. high is suitable. You can accentuate a circle of one item, as in Fig. 6-1, but I think it is more interesting to at least alternate things. If you are limited in your material, consider the ring in Fig. 6-3. Its central pattern uses only one kind of cone, but every other one is upside down. If the sizes of the cones prevent you from completing the pattern symmetrically, vary the design by making a focal point at the end with something altogether different. Even when you start out with concentric circles of the same types of items, a really good job of filling in the interstices will nearly hide this foundation.

Another way to begin is to make three groupings of the same items spaced symmetrically around the ring (see the candle ring in Figs. 1-9 and 1-10). Then fill in between the groupings with other larger items. Much of this first layer may be covered eventually, but the strength will be there, as well as a foundation on which to glue the finishing touches. Lay the basic items out around the ring first to get an idea of the effect before you begin gluing. Use enough glue for each item so it will stick firmly. I find that putting some nuts in the base layer makes for more interesting contrast, because they shine so well after the glaze is applied. Often you can place a nut between two cones, letting it stick out just a fraction beyond the edge of the ring. Pecans, almonds, Brazil nuts, hickory nuts, and big filberts are especially good. One year we had a supply of chestnuts that had failed to mature. They were nearly all shell and had curves that allowed us to place them in the outer layers of candle rings for a really striking effect. Allow the foundation layer to dry well before continuing.

Now you must visualize what the completed ring will look like. It ought to be at least 1 in. higher than the top of the Styrofoam, and it should form a somewhat tapered mound rather than having absolutely straight sides. Every chink should be filled in. First glue on items about the size of a nickel and a dime: acorns and their empty cups, poppy seed heads, perennial bachelor's-button heads, day-lily pods, larch cones, or hemlock cones, for example. Colum-

bine seed pods, althea pods, and the like, which have interesting openings but fragile bodies, can be slipped in to fill spaces in such a way that stronger items protect them while allowing their outside patterns to show. You can put these secondary things on in some kind of sequence or randomly in spaces where they fit.

Next you graduate to even smaller fillers: beechnuts, wisteria seeds, cherry pits, arborvitae cones, balloon-flower capsules, immature acorns and pine cones, rhododendron seed capsules. And lastly, to the very smallest things which will fit into the least discernible cracks: lilac seed heads, deutzia and philadelphus pods, tiny chamaecyparis cones, or sprigs of mountain mint heads. Check Chapter 1 for lists of raw materials that you can gather.

The real art of making a candle ring lies in this filling-in process, and while it can be tedious, it creates a wonderfully interesting effect when done with care. Most rings are viewed close-up, after all, and I cannot emphasize enough how important this technique is for success.

When you are satisfied that no holes are left anywhere around the ring, allow the glue to dry well overnight, and then spray thoroughly with two coats of clear glaze. To protect your furniture, you can then glue a piece of felt to the bottom of the ring if you wish. It can be cut either in a ring to fit the original Styrofoam or in a complete circle so that even the candle rests upon the felt.

A candle 3 in. in diameter will stand without support in one of these rings. If you use a smaller size, push some crumpled tissue paper around its base to prevent tipping. Most of these candles are about 6 in. tall, and a ring that is 1–2 in. high is quite in proportion. If you prefer a stubby candle, make your ring no higher than 1 in.

Variation: I have a favorite glass candle that is 9 in. tall, which looked quite silly in the normal candle ring. I cut a ring 6¼ in. in outside diameter out of Styrofoam 1¼ in. thick. Its hole is only 3 in. in diameter to fit the special candle. Around the outer edge of the ring I glued large beech burrs pointing outward so that the true diameter at the bottom of the ring became nearly 8 in. I built up the ring itself to a height of 3 in. by gluing on an unseen extra layer of base materials (see Fig. C-36). You can custom-make a ring for any odd-sized candle by experimenting with slightly larger or smaller rings, but remember that the larger the ring is in diameter, the higher it must be to keep the proportions right.

Variation: you can trim the outer edge of the smal-

Fig. 6-7. Two very different shapes of candle rings on exactly the same sized base. The size and placement of raw materials creates great variety. Note how readily they could be adapted for use as small wreaths.

ler ring as detailed in the recipe with small bunches of sea lavender fastened to the Styrofoam with continuous wiring. The ring itself can then be decorated with strawflowers and other softer materials, as in Fig. C-30. You should be able to identify thistles, tiny clematis seed heads, stokesia calyxes, and globe amaranths, among other things, in it. You could just as easily bind fresh perennial statice around the edge. It would be a very suitable combination to use seashells for the body with a ring trimmed with either of these. For that matter, you can even trim the outer edge with seashells, but this becomes a very long process; only a bit of the edge can be done at one time, since the shells cannot be pinned in place. The ring must be propped on its side so a section at a time can dry securely. It is also much harder to fill in the interstices, because the shells are angular and inflexible. Perhaps I did not have a large enough selection of raw materials; if you live by the sea, you might not have this problem.

Variation: almost any of these candle rings, except those which have been built up very high, can be used as a small hanging wreath (see the rings in Fig. 6-7). Use thin ribbon for bows or back them with a cardboard disk covered with colored foil for still another effect.

Bobeche

Materials:

Styrofoam ring 3 in. in diameter, ½ in. thick
   or
Styrofoam ring 4 in. in diameter, 1 in. thick
floral tape
white glue and dip pot
assorted small cones, pods, nuts, etc.
clear glaze spray

Originally, a bobeche was a simple cupped ring put on the socket of a candlestick to catch the drippings. It evolved into an elaborate object with crystal drops and other fancy trimmings. With the advent of dripless candles, it became solely a decoration. Nowadays, gift shops are full of gaudy bobeches, exploding with plastic grapes and ivy leaves. Some are quite lovely, but many are blatantly artificial.

You can make a much more subtle bobeche yourself from the bounties of nature. Styrofoam disks in the smaller sizes are available, or you can cut your own from a sheet with a serrated knife. For the ordinary single candlestick, which holds a candle up to 1 in. in diameter, your bobeche should be made in the smaller dimensions in the recipe. A very large candlestick requires the larger size. The centers of the disk must be removed, again with the knife, or with a hot cookie cutter if you have a tiny one. Measure your candle and make the hole just a little bigger than the diameter of the candle; make sure, however, that the hole is not so large that the disk falls down the holder or tips around the candle. Most antique candlesticks have some fullness at the top to hold a bobeche, but many modern ones are very slim. If necessary, make a template from a piece of thin cardboard first to test the fit. When you have cut out the Styrofoam ring, wrap it all around with concentric layers of floral tape to give extra strength, just as for the wreaths and candle rings.

Decorate the outside edge of the ring by gluing small cones or pods to it as closely together as possible. Tiny hemlock cones, American beech burrs, or very small spruce cones are good choices for this. The bobeche in Figs. 6-8–6-13 is trimmed with flowers made from cutting small spruce cones in thirds and using only the two flat sections. I could just as easily have used only the tips or a combination of the flat sections and the rounder tips.

Make sure before you start even the edges that you have enough raw materials. Nothing is worse than to run out and be unable to finish the second of a pair. I usually make the two together, and I deliberately glue the same item at the same time on the tops of both bobeches.

It is difficult to duplicate the effect of something hanging from the bobeche with cones and pods. The old crystal bobeches used drops, and the artificial ones of today use tiny bunches of fake grapes. I have found that you can glue some small spruce cones on the edges with their tips pointing down; secure them with pins until the glue dries (see Fig. 6-14). If you don't like that effect, you can soften the edges with

Figs. 6-8, 6-9, 6-10, 6-11, 6-12, and 6-13. The life story of a bobeche. 6-8. The outside edge is trimmed with flowers made from slices of small spruce cones. 6-9. Larger items are glued on top first. 6-10. All interstices have been carefully filled in and small sprigs of pearly everlasting added

temporarily. 6-11. Some gilded holly leaves we stuck into cracks here and there but were no glued in place. 6-12. Holly leaves and pearly everlasting were removed, and small pieces o perennial statice were inserted temporarily. 6- Temporary decoration of small fresh-picked juniper sprigs for a green note.

Fig. 6-14. Bobeche on a bottle for working purposes shows how small cones can be glued to the edges to give a hanging effect.

Figs. 6-15 and 6-16. Top and side views of two very different bobeches. Left: this is made of very small magnolia leaves glued in place. Right: this is trimmed with sprigs of sea-lavender and assorted small cones.

curved gilded holly leaves or sprigs of perennial statice. Or you can temporarily add small twigs of a graceful evergreen like arborvitae or white pine when you use the bobeches.

Figs. 6-8–6-13 show various stages of making a bobeche, then the same basic bobeche with some temporary variations to give it a different look. The holly leaves, pearly everlasting, statice, and evergreens are not glued on, but rather their stems are inserted into tiny chinks in the bobeche.

Like the candle ring, the bobeche will be viewed close-up. After you have glued the larger items on the top, you must fill in the interstices very carefully. Vary the shapes, sizes, and colors of the things you use to add interest. Although I try to duplicate the basic edging and to place the important items in the same sequence for both members of a pair, I work separately on the interstices. I do, however, trim both pieces with the same small items, even if not in exactly the same spots.

One way to work a bobeche is to stick a candle stub of the right diameter in a glass bottle and balance the bobeche on the bottle while you work. This gives you an idea of proportion and also ensures that no item is glued too close to the inner hole so the candle won't fit when you're finished. You can also do the work

right on the holder, but always make sure to clean up the inevitable drops of glue before they mar the holder.

It is somewhat tedious to work on a bobeche, simply because your fingers seem too big. I find that tweezers help a lot. The shrub border is a handy source of many usable items for this small-scale work. Seed capsules from common decoratives like lilac, deutzia, philadelphus, witch-hazel, arborvitae, rhododendron, and pussy willows are among the handiest trimmings for a bobeche.

If you have certain favorite colors in your dining room, you can work some strawflowers into a bobeche too. Since this decoration will get a certain amount of handling (if only when you change candles), do not use anything that is very fragile unless it can be worked between two sturdier items to protect it.

A pair of bobeches is a very satisfying sort of decoration to have around because it can be used so often. It is also something that you can make without having a large quantity of raw materials at hand. I store the smaller sizes of many items like sweet-gum balls and pine cones separately just to have them ready for bobeches. Along with candle rings, they make favorite gifts too.

Candle Log
Materials:
    pretty log 3–4 in. in diameter, 6–12 in. long
    white glue
    clear glaze spray
    assorted lichens, cones, etc.
    felt (optional)

You can substitute "interesting" for "pretty" in the description of the log base in the recipe. White birch, gray beech, shiny black cherry, and mottled green and brown sycamore are my favorites, but there are many other kinds of trees with bark that is excitingly rough or sleekly smooth. The log should come from a tree that is newly cut or fallen, because you don't want any insect life or rot. If you like an older log with lichens naturally formed on it, spray it with insecticide and leave it in a tightly closed plastic bag for a week as a precaution.

The cut ends of the log should be neat and may need a little sanding. A coat of clear glaze spray on the ends helps to seal them. But first you must make sure that your log will sit steadily so it cannot tip with a lighted candle. Sometimes you can find a small limb with a few branchlets protruding at just the right angle to act as a brace; cut them off neatly so only a few inches extend beyond the log, and you're all set.

More likely you will have to flatten one side. Mark the end of the log with a cross so that the outside diameter is divided in quarters. Then stand the log on end, take careful aim with your hand ax or hatchet, and whomp down on the log between two adjacent arms of the cross. Once the ax is in firmly, you can lift the log up with it and bang on the ground until you split off that piece. Use a plane or a few more short strokes with the ax to smooth your flat side. Glue a piece of felt on it to protect your funiture if you wish.

In the top of the log, you are going to bore one or more holes about 1 in. deep for the candles. Decide what sizes of candles will go best with the log. You can have just one about 2 in. in diameter, or as many as three regular tapers, or two tapers and one slightly larger. Mark the exact size of the hole desired on the bark at the right spot. Most hand drills have a large auger, which you can use to make the hole. It is much easier if you can put the log in a vise first, but you can hold it steady with your feet too.

For a big hole, you'll have to drill several smaller ones close together, then neaten the opening with your jackknife. The candle should fit snuggly into the hole, but you can use melted wax or floral clay to give it an extra anchor.

Keep the decorations on your log simple. You can glue on a few dried leaves or a piece of lichen placed so that it looks as if it were growing from the log. Or you can make a grouping of a sweet-gum ball, acorn cup, or small cone with some moss. Keep the decorations near the top and center of the log to face down the candles. Often these touches can be used to hide any scratches that you may have made around the holes.

Variation: if you have access to a saw mill, you can pick up an interesting slab of wood which will fill your needs, and it will already have a flat side from the mill.

Fig. 6-17. Close-up of the center of a mantel decoration.

You can cut a slab from a much bigger log to make a flatter centerpiece than the whole small log in the first recipe. Make sure the piece is deep enough to allow you to drill a decent hole for the candle. Decorate as desired with cones and pods. With a larger flat surface, you can make a much more elaborate arrangement around the candle holes than with the small log. It will also look in proportion to a much fatter candle than the small log could possibly handle.

Variation: weathered driftwood pieces also make excellent candle holders. Choose one that sits securely on one side, however, for driftwood is not easy to work. Some pieces are quite soft, but others are like iron. Carve the hole for the candle carefully with a small jackknife so that you don't break the wood. You can also buy screw-type metal candle holders in craft shops to attach the candle if all else fails. Seashells, dried seaweed, statice, and sea lavender are particularly appropriate raw materials for decorating driftwood. Pieces that look like old roots make some of the most interesting candle holders.

Mantelpieces
Materials:
    large sheet of Styrofoam ½–1 in. thick
    plywood or heavy corrugated cardboard
    floral tape
    white glue and dip pot
    assorted cones, pods, nuts, etc.
    clear glaze spray

In any home with a fireplace, the mantel becomes a focal point of the holiday decorations. You can make a very simple natural arrangement with a few pieces of evergreen foliage, some loose cones and nuts placed among the branches, and perhaps a few special figurines or family heirlooms.

There may come a time, however, when you want something more elaborate. These mantelpieces can be used along with just a few very small bits of greenery, or they can act as a backdrop for whatever else you wish to put on the shelf or to hang above it. If you have no fireplace, this decoration can also be used effectively on a bookcase or at the back of a long table against a wall.

From the Styrofoam, cut an isosceles triangle that measures 36 in. long on the base and is about 3 in. high at the mid-point. Then cut another triangle of the same size from either plywood or heavy cardboard. Glue the two triangles together, weight down with some heavy books, and leave to dry overnight. I made my first mantelpiece from Styrofoam alone and found that it was not strong enough to bear the weight of the cones and nuts that I glued to it. Whenever I move it, I must support it carefully to keep it from breaking. Since this will be a decoration you can cherish for many years, make it even stronger by wrapping it from one end to the other in overlapping floral tape, just as with the heritage wreath in Chapter 2.

The trimming also follows the same technique, but attach the edging cones or pods only to the upper edge, since it sits on the shelf on its bottom edge. I decided to make my piece symmetrical. I worked out a special design for the center, using three huge seed pods from a *Magnolia grandiflora*, velvety green wisteria pods, gilded holly leaves, and some crossed oak twigs full of empty acorn cups. Fig. 6-17 shows how these diverse materials were worked together. I have never used this mantelpiece without placing greens

Fig. 6-18. The mantelpiece has a symmetrical
design.

Fig. 6-19. Symmetry of another mantelpiece on
either side of the center.

(usually white pine) behind it and on the sides, but I wanted to show it alone in its entirety to give you an idea of how to make one for yourself. You can see the center of another one, with a martynia bird perched at the peak, in Fig. 6-19. Once the centers were complete, I worked outwards on either side, trying to glue on the same items in the same sequence. One half isn't exactly like the other, of course, but it is close. Once the glue is dry, the whole piece should be sprayed with several coats of clear glaze.

Variation: after you have cut out the Styrofoam triangle, divide it at the center to form two right triangles of exactly the same size. Back and wrap them for strength, as with the previous piece. Instead of a focal point, use something special at the mid-point of your mantel. It can be a favorite statue, a vase of greens, a big candle holder, or anything else that your fancy dictates. Then arrange the two decorated triangles on either side with their right angles to the center. When you decorate them, edge both the upper side of the triangle and the straight vertical edge, but leave the bottom edge empty to give it a place to sit. Make a careful attempt to decorate the two triangles as exactly alike as possible.

7
pictures, bellpulls, plaques, and a surprise

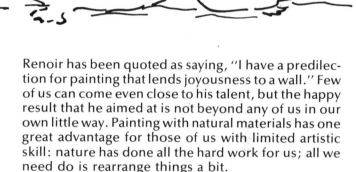

Drawing 17. Simple drawing for a seed picture made with real branches and cattails. White squash seeds give the effect of feathers on the ducks.

Renoir has been quoted as saying, "I have a predilection for painting that lends joyousness to a wall." Few of us can come even close to his talent, but the happy result that he aimed at is not beyond any of us in our own little way. Painting with natural materials has one great advantage for those of us with limited artistic skill: nature has done all the hard work for us; all we need do is rearrange things a bit.

Actually we are going to consider art forms so simple that Renoir would hardly think them worth mentioning, but you can have a delightful interlude and preserve some of the best of your garden or vacation memories at the same time. If the result is less than perfect, there is yet a satisfaction in the attempt itself. And practice does produce some improvement.

Strictly speaking, the wreaths and two-dimensional trees described earlier are meant to be hung on walls too. The subjects of this section are closer to pictures or tapestries. Indeed, one way to get ideas if you feel somewhat of an amateur at all this is to thumb through a needlework catalog. Much of what has been designed for embroidery or crewelwork is highly adaptable for working with natural materials. Notice how some designs feature a straight, long line or a sweeping curve. Try to obtain the same effect with what you have at hand. In Drawing 17, which is a rough diagram for a seed picture, I have indicated pussy willows and cattails for that very reason. I wanted a bold line for the picture, and these natural materials hold up well, so they seemed ideal for the pond area where both are found.

You need not master all of the artist's techniques, but if you begin to put together pictures or plaques from some of the embroidery patterns, you will be using proportion and line without consciously realizing it. The main thing is to enjoy yourself, so forget about whether you are violating rules. You can always take refuge in calling yourself a primitive, and look where that got Grandma Moses.

The butterfly hanging in Fig. C-31 was supposed to have a series of soft curves created by the sea oats. It didn't quite work out that way, but I still like it. My flower picture (Fig. C-28) was intended to achieve still another kind of balance with lines more or less radiating from a central point. If I'm not afraid to offer my creations for public ridicule by experts, why should you give a second thought to what you do for your own pleasure?

If you are clever with a needle, you're way ahead of the game, because you can make some truly beautiful things by combining this skill with your natural materials. Some effects are quite difficult when you are limited to items like branches, cones, and pods, even if you have access to pressed leaves and flowers. The water for the ducks, for example, could be suggested perfectly with a few lines of yarn here and there, and it would really be prettier than the seeds. I will merely outline some of the basic techniques that I have found handy for various wall decorations. Many of you will range far beyond me in no time.

Wall Plaques

Materials:
  wood base
  background material (optional)
  hanger
  white glue and dip pot
  assorted dry material
  clear glaze spray

Bases useful for making plaques come in a wide range. You can cut your own from plywood and stain

or paint it, or you can buy plaque bases in hobby shops. Often they come with a hanger, and they may even have fancy routed edges. The slab piles at a saw mill are another good source. They will have flat backs, and many are thin enough to use for this purpose. If a piece is too long for your plaque, it is easily shortened with a saw. Look for thin slabs of gray beech, shiny fruit wood, any of the birches, or barkless weathered pieces with interesting grain. Once I found a thin slab of what could only have been an old telephone pole. Its rough gouged surface made a great plaque. Old barns and buildings yield fine weathered boards; sometimes you can find wood that has aged to a soft silver. Flat driftwood is a real treasure for this work.

A few knotholes or imperfections in the bark pattern do not preclude its use for a plaque; they can even add interest to your final design. Make sure that the wood is clean and free of insects; dry for a few days if necessary. If you can find nothing else that suits your idea, cut a piece of plywood to the desired shape and size, and cover it by gluing on some burlap or similar material in the color you want. For finished edges, cut enough material to overlap the plywood, and glue to the back side. Miter the corners for a good fit.

Before you decorate the plaque, decide what kind of hanger to use. If you are going to glue it on, you can do that after you have finished, but if you are going to screw or nail it on, you should attach it beforehand. Make sure that the hanger is strong enough to support the weight of the plaque and whatever else you will put on it; thin plywood needs much less sturdy a hanger than my telephone pole, for example. The clerks at hardware stores are very helpful. Take your plaque along to show them.

Having disposed of these preliminaries, lay the plaque on your work surface, and play around with the materials you have at hand. The plaque in Fig. 7-2 contains a wide variety of dried materials to give it interest. The color, form, size, and texture of the items are all important, but don't use only one of everything. Repeat some articles, perhaps in different sizes. Odd numbers of one thing are often more pleasing, but you can have formal balance on either

Fig. 7-3. A piece of razor-clam shell makes a holder for sea oats and strawflowers on a piece of driftwood.

side of the mid-point too. That particular plaque has an irregular piece of sycamore bark glued down first. This adds interest to the plain background and helps to connect the long stems of the redwood cones to the mass of material at the bottom. The plaque in Fig. C-26 is mainly made of dried citrus fruit skins cut into various flower forms. These have a uniformity of substance and color that holds them together.

I often draw the general shape of my design on the plaque first with a light pencil line. It might be a stretched-out S, an oval, a triangle, or just a straight line. The design depends somewhat on whether your plaque is round, square, or rectangular. You can tell a sort of story or just lay out a pleasing pattern of materials. Arrange the items at hand along the guideline in different ways until you get a design that you like. Generally the larger, heavier-looking things should go near the bottom or the middle, depending on what sort of design you have, but you will want some little things here and there to fill in the spaces and draw it all together. Make your design two-dimensional rather than flat; put some things partially under others, or stick some out at angles.

Now you can either remove everything and put it carefully beside you in approximately the same sequence, or you can remove just the top things and begin gluing those that go closest to the plaque surface. Continue until everything is in place and leave overnight to dry. Then give the plaque two good coats of clear glaze spray.

Your plaque need not have a regular geometric shape. The one in Fig. 7-3 was made with a piece of long, thin driftwood. The piece of razor-clam shell used to suggest a container for the flowers and grasses is in fine proportion to the plaque itself. A scallop shell would be as lovely on a wider plaque.

Variation: white birch bark is hard to come by, but once in a while you may find a log or a fallen tree. Even though the wood may be rotting, the bark is nearly indestructible. Make a slit along the whole length of the log, and peel off the bark carefully (or soak the entire log until this is possible). Scrub the underside of the bark to remove any debris or wood. If you then soak the bark overnight, it will usually be pliable enough to roll flat. Shake off excess water,

and weight it down quite heavily. Dry in a warm spot as quickly as possible so that no mold will form. Then glue it to a backing of thin plywood, and it makes a most interesting background for an arrangement.

Variation: with a wicker basket or a cornucopia, you can make an altogether different kind of two-dimensional plaque. Carefully cut the cornucopia in half, or slice off about a third of the basket. Glue the cut side to the plaque. When it is firmly in place, fill the bottom of the opening created between the plaque and the wicker with crumpled tissue paper. Now arrange pine cones, pods, and nuts so that the container appears to be overflowing with nature's bounty. A few dried halves of orange, lime, or lemon skin can be slipped behind the outer material to look as if there were fruits in the harvest too. If desired, the handle of the basket or a heavy piece of rope can be glued to the backing before filling. You can also glue some pressed autumn leaves behind the main design to add irregularity to the design.

Framed Plaque or Shadow Box
Materials:
    deep wood frame
    cardboard or other backing
    background material
    hanger
    white glue and dip pot
    assorted dried materials
    clear glaze spray

The frame in Fig. C-28 is just about 1½ in. deep, and I think that this is the bare minimum for this type of plaque. A shallower frame would be overwhelmed by the weight of the items inside, for you are again making a picture in two dimensions. In a sense, this is a shadow box, but it is easier to construct, because it is not closed in. You could of course buy a shadow-box frame, in which case your plaque would last much longer. But many of us have spare ordinary frames around, and this plaque is meant to last a season or two and then to be replaced by something new. Its contents will not have cost much in time or money.

What you use for backing depends on what will fit in the back of the frame. The easiest way to do it is to

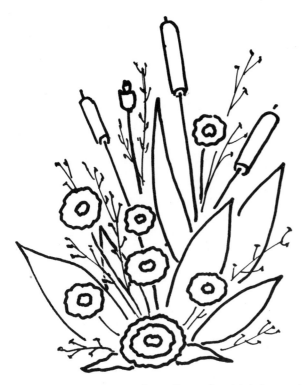

cover a heavy piece of cardboard, which is cut just a fraction smaller than the inset provided for it in the back of the frame, with natural-color, self-sticking burlap. You have only to peel off the protecting paper to apply it. You can also glue on fabric just as neatly. The color of the background depends entirely on your own taste, the raw materials you have to work with, and the color of the frame itself; all should be in harmony. If you cover the backing with fabric, make sure the piece is big enough to tuck under so no raw edges will show. Miter the corners of the material for a good fit.

Drawing 18 shows a competent artist's rendition of the very rough sketch I had made before starting the plaque itself. What I wanted to do, and what I suggest for you, is to determine the main placement of the items to be used. Once I had decided this, I began gluing the first layer of things and gradually worked out until everything was in place. Even with tacky glue, it was necessary to weight some items down for a few hours so they held well before the next layer was started. For the large leaves and cattails, I applied the glue to the item before putting it in place, but the grasses were too fine for that treatment, so I figured where they were to go, put the glue on the burlap first and then pressed the grasses onto that. Use glue

sparingly so it won't show, remove any inadvertent drops immediately, and keep the whole background absolutely clean. I kept tweezers handy so that if a flower or a grass shed a speck, I could remove it before it stuck.

The leaves in my picture are from the common mullein, a roadside weed which I had gathered earlier and pressed, but you can use any kind of dried leaf or fern. It doesn't even have to be pressed flat, as long as it can be glued into the picture the way you want. All materials should be completely dry before gluing, however.

If you plan a fan-shaped arrangement such as mine, remember that you must cover the raw stems at the bottom when you have finished. Many of mine are hidden by a covering layer of material, but the sprays of statice at the bottom were intended to screen what is behind them. I allowed a little statice to extend over the frame, because it looked so graceful. I could just as well have hidden the stems at the bottom with something solid, such as pine cones. When you are all done, give the plaque several light coats of clear glaze spray. It will not harm the burlap.

A plaque like this can also contain a pattern of cones and pods. Arrange them in a soft S along the length of the frame, for example. The only difference between the framed and the plain plaque is that the frame acts as a protection of sorts so that you can use more elaborate designs and more fragile materials. Because no one can look sidewise into the design, you can also build it up in layers without worrying about what might show from the sides. The framed plaque also looks somewhat more formal and finished.

If you prefer to use a regular shadow-box frame, proceed just as above, but do not allow any of the material to extend beyond the groove where the front glass is set.

Seed Mosaics
Materials:
    plywood outline, frame, or plaque
    white glue and dip pot
    tweezers
    assorted dried materials and seeds

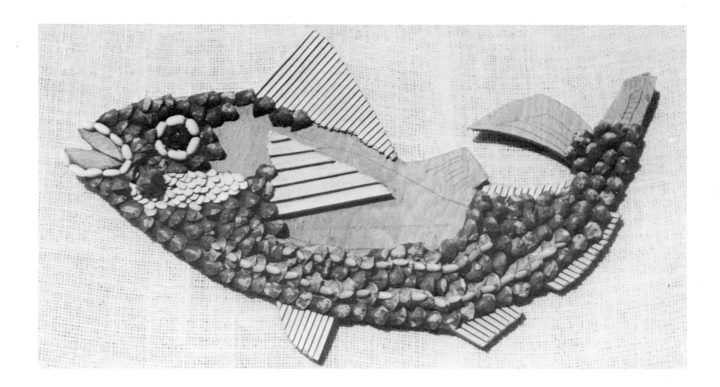

balsa wood
clear glaze spray

I do not have the patience to make true seed mosaics, as you can easily tell from the unfinished fish in Fig. 7-4. Gluing all those tiny things in place does nothing to improve my disposition, and when I do finish, the results seem so static. If you add other materials besides seeds, however, you can jazz it up a bit. Texture is very important in this kind of work, and that is the main contribution of an expanded list of raw materials.

Soft balsa wood is especially handy, and it can be purchased in various sizes and thicknesses. It also takes paint and stain well. It is very appropriate for the fins of the fish. I put the tiny discarded stems of a medium-sized strawflower between the balsa strips to give the ribbing effect and used wider strips to differentiate the big swim fin. The smaller, thinner piece of balsa can be cut with a jackknife or heavy scissors. The lips of the fish were carved from slices of avocado seed, but you could make these with balsa too.

The fish scales are actually the clipped scales of eastern white pine cones. Two lines of orange cantaloupe seeds add interest to the lower body,

and the gills are summer-squash seeds. White bean seeds outline the eye of black seeds. People who do much of this work often dye their seeds. My photographer's assistant told me that she once made a rooster completely from dyed rice and nearly went blind in the process. I would suggest that if coloring is necessary, it would be easier to glue on the pieces first and then touch up with a fine brush and acrylic paint.

My fish was cut from thin plywood with a coping saw. You can make an outline of almost anything in the same way. First draw the pattern freehand on a large sheet of paper, or find something to trace. Children's coloring books are a good source of simple outline figures. Animals, birds, and butterflies are particularly effective in outline. Transfer to the wood with carbon paper, then cut out.

Seed mosaics can be made on a regularly shaped background just as easily as in outline. Cut a plywood rectangle, for example, and then draw a simple picture on it. A formalist will then fill in the entire picture with seeds, using packets of garden seeds, as well as what's available in the grocery store. But this is so static. Take the drawing of the ducks; washed squash seeds dry a good white color for their feathers, but I

Fig. 7-4. Balsa wood fins add interest to this seed mosaic of a fish.

Drawing 19. Seed daisies are one of the easiest flower forms to make.

Squash seeds and split peas

Cantaloupe seeds and popcorn

would probably add to the interest of the figure by trimming a bleached milkweed pod to suggest a folded wing. I have already indicated that the pussy willows and cattails can be themselves. You could outline the waves of the pond at the top with green split peas, continuing this pattern all the way through to get an approximation of water, and you could suggest the land with tannish mustard seeds. I assume that you would spread a patch of glue on the background first and then stick the seeds in it with the tweezers. Personally, I would go mad from the tedium long before it was finished.

Unless you have a sick relative whom you must keep in bed over a long period (that's about the best excuse I can think of), why not use more imagination? Buy some remnants or delve into your sewing scraps for plain-colored felt, velvet, linen, and other materials that have body and texture.

We are, after all, dealing with a fairly simple idea. The duck picture needs three background colors at most: gray, green, or blue for the water; brown or green for the land; blue for the sky. Cut a piece of fabric with a wavy top for the water. Cut the piece for the land on a slant to suggest a hill rather than straight across. Glue these pieces on the backing before you start the rest of the picture. Use carbon paper to draw the ducks and position the weeds. Then fill in the ducks with the seeds, and paste on the larger items. Use a few groups of seeds to suggest clumps of grass on the land, some more to outline a wave here and there in the water. To my way of thinking, you'll have a much more interesting picture to look at, and the textures of the principal features will stand out much more strikingly.

Going a step farther, if you use cloth material as a background, you can fashion all manner of pictures with rocks, cones, and sticks, as well as seeds. Relieved of the tedium of filling in the backgrounds, most children have a ball with this sort of project. Suggest a story for them to tell, help them gather some raw materials, and let their imaginations take over. Pumpkin seeds from a jack-o'-lantern can be washed and dried to start your youngster off on some fun for a winter day. Drawing 19 shows how some of

the very commonest seeds can be used to create flowers, but these are just starting points. Squash seeds can be glued on a triangle so they overlap to make a snow-covered evergreen tree. A cherry pit makes a perfect baseball, a navy bean a football; a red kidney bean and some tiny sticks becomes a great bug. You can see for yourself where all this might lead.

Hangings
Materials:
    heavy burlap or similar material
    edging (optional)
    two wooden dowels
    curtain weights (optional)
    white glue and dip pot
    round shoestrings
    assorted dried material
    clear glaze spray

For me the hanging made with natural materials is one of the most enjoyable and satisfying projects in this entire book. It can be made in every conceivable size and adapted to so many different uses and places. I like it best when it is not too small. Then you can make bold designs with larger materials.

Fig. 7-5. Seashells at the bottom of the hanging help to weight it down and to hide the raw ends of statice and sea oats. They are also ecologically accurate, since statice and sea oats are often found growing near the ocean. Monarch and viceroy butterflies at the top of the hanging are frequent migratory visitors to ocean areas.

Heavy velvet or almost any plain-colored upholstering fabric can be utilized, but I prefer stiffened burlap. It can be bought in a variety of colors in fabric stores, hobby shops, and sometimes in hardware or wallpaper stores. One type has been stiffened by some kind of process; another is self-sticking, and the backing gives it a fine body. This latter kind can still be cut with sharp shears; leave the paper backing on to give it heft. With most materials you need to make a thin, turned-over hem on both side edges to keep it from raveling, but with the self-stick burlap it is possible to omit this step. Experiment with the material; often you can glue the side hem in, especially if you are going to cover it with an edging.

Let's consider the butterfly hanging in Fig. C-31 to illustrate the whole process. I wanted a long, narrow piece to fit in an odd corner by the fireplace. Finished, it measures 36 in. long and just under 6 in. wide, but I allowed about 3 in. more in length. This gave me extra material for top and bottom hems, in which the wooden dowels are inserted. I measured the dowel in the material first to make sure it would fit. One long edge was selvage, but I turned over the other a fraction to prevent raveling before I applied the edging strip. I sewed the latter on, but I could just as well have glued it. I have made many very attractive hangings without side edgings, but I do prefer the effect that these give. The edging extends on both top and bottom around to the back, again to prevent raveling.

I chose the dark green and the orange monarch and viceroy butterflies to harmonize with the colors in the living room. Because the hanging would be free to the air, I removed the butterfly bodies (which attract insects) very carefully and cut substitutes from the brown pod of a honey locust tree. Their heads are pine cone seeds. The antennae were carefully pasted on at the end. Check how the wings are attached before removing them so your butterfly will look natural.

I decided to make the backbone of the design with gracefully curving sea oats, but I could not use a whole branch; it simply would not stay in place correctly. I ended up snipping small branchlets of oats, removing a few capsules on some, adding a few more

on others with glue. After laying out the general design of the oats, I glued each part separately, then weighted it down until it dried. The big butterfly in the middle hides the raw end of one oat stem. The insects were not added until all the oats were firmly in place. Snap clothespins are very handy for holding things in place until the glue dries.

The statice and seashells at the bottom serve a double purpose. Not only do they hide the raw bottom of the other sea oat stem, but they also weight down the hanging. Even with the dowel inside the bottom hem, you may find that the weight is not sufficient for the piece to hang straight. In that case, glue a couple of curtain weights on the back at the bottom.

Before you start working on a hanging, find or make a shallow cardboard box that will hold it absolutely flat. It is not possible to make a hanging in one sitting, and you do not want to move it without support while one step is drying. Incidentally, if you have fabric that you intend to use for a hanging, always roll it rather than folding it; deep creases are often impossible to remove.

Before slipping the top dowel into place, I carved a groove into both ends to hold the shoestring tie, but you could fasten it with a knot too. The bottom dowel

Figs. 7-6 and 7-7. Left: the dowel on top helps to keep the hanging flat. Right: a shoestring alone has been threaded through the top hem. This latter method will work only for narrow hangings which are light in weight.

does not show, but notice that the upper one must be a bit longer than the width of the hanging so you can fasten the tie line. You could use almost any kind of twine, but the shoestrings come in various lengths, and they have finished ends. For a narrow hanging it is possible to just thread the shoestring through the top hem and hang it without a dowel, but the wooden support helps to keep it rigid. This point can be important if some of the raw materials are fragile like the butterfly wings. I broke the top one while trying to thumbtack the hanging for the photograph.

After everything is glued in place, give the whole thing, burlap and all, several light coats of clear glaze spray. This not only helps to preserve it but also makes dusting much easier. Just reverse the vacuum cleaner over it a few times a year.

Your hanging can be much wider and shorter than the one illustrated. The only difference is that the dowels must be longer. The wider the hanging, the more you need to weight the bottom so it hangs straight. With a wider area, you have almost infinite latitude in your materials but the simplest designs are usually best.

One clever idea is to trim a branch and press it so it lies flat when placed on the background. Then glue some small pine cone owls (as described in Chapter 8) on it. A leaf or two here and there and some cones and nuts to weight the bottom, and you have a very different decoration. One of the quickest and most effective hangings I ever made had a central line of long wheat straws with a few pieces of grass that had dried more or less green. These we glued on first and held down with books and pins until all of them were firmly stuck to the burlap. Then all around the center I glued small autumn-colored leaves, as if they were falling in mid-air from the trees. I stuck a few more leaves at the bottom, on top of which I glued some nuts, small cones, and odd pods and burrs. Near the top was a dragonfly quickly glued together, in a similar fashion made of maple key wings and a pod body. This hanging completely captured the spirit of fall.

You can use grasses, cattails, branches of broom or pussy willows, dried fern fronds, or pieces of twigs for the strong lines. A slender piece of grapevine, cut while green, can be pressed and dried complete with tendrils for a most interesting backbone of a hanging. A small branch from a tree like the dogwood, which has a horizontal growth pattern, can be pressed flat too.

Or you can make a series of similar arrangements along the whole length of a long hanging with cones

Fig. 7-8. Bellpull hanging actually has a tiny bell at the bottom. This picture shows how small pieces of dried material can be glued in place to give a definite line to a design.

or strawflowers. We made an unusual one by arranging dried red peppers to look like poinsettias. On a natural burlap background with a few pressed green leaves, this provided a great holiday decoration, but the owner loved it so much that she kept it hanging all year. The bellpull hanging in Fig. 7-8 has a long series of soft curves as its backbone. Small pieces of annual and perennial statice were glued along the curves, and strawflowers were added later for centers of interest. This is a great opportunity for the embroidery expert to stitch in a central leader of greenery, which can then be decorated with almost anything colorful. Pressed flowers and leaves are naturals for hangings, but you can just as easily utilize pods and cones.

Variation: when you cut the material for a long, thin hanging, snip off the corners to bring the bottom to a point. Then fasten a tassel, a tiny bell, or a pretty pull of some kind to that spot. Presto, a bell-pull hanging.

Variation: use stick curtains instead of fabric for the backing. You can cut them with a wire cutter or pruning shears to whatever length and width you want. You can put a dowel in the top either by folding over a hem and securing it in several places with thin wire or by running the dowel through the hangers already provided at the top of the curtain. Or you can use the metal curtain hangers that have a loop at the top and a pincher at the bottom; secure the pincher to your hanging and run a wide dowel through the loops. Do not glue very fragile material to such a backing, because it tends to fold very easily.

Variation: an attractive way to hang up your yardstick is merely a variation of the long, thin hanging. Cut two pieces of unstiffened burlap about 3–4 in. wide; one should be just 36 in. long, the other 40 in. Turn under 1 in. at the top of the shorter piece, and sew the pieces together at the bottoms and sides; leave the top open to make a pocket for the yardstick, and make sure that the hemmed edge of the shorter piece is on the inside. Hem the top of the longer piece, and put in a dowel to hang it with. Decorate the short side with fairly durable dried materials.

Stiffened burlap is sometimes sold in rolls 3 in. wide, and it has selvages on both edges. With this you can sew the two pieces together without having to

Drawing 20. Naturalist's frame filled with more interesting treasures than piles of seeds.

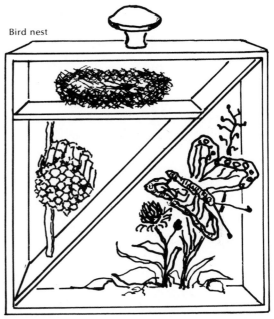

Bird nest

Wasp nest   Butterfly on dried flowers

turn afterward. Use either the machine or sew by hand with yarn. The seams will show with this method, so use a contrasting color if you want to make them part of the overall design.

Naturalist's Frame

Materials:

    compartmented wooden frame
    white glue
    assorted dry materials

For a while every gift shop had a selection of frames filled with collections of different-colored seeds. Frankly, they didn't appeal to me much—I'd rather plant my seeds than look at them—but I was willing to let my daughters enjoy them. Until I went past one day and saw life stirring in the frame!

Anyone who has worked with a seed or food company will admit that keeping wildlife out of the raw stock is an uphill job. Most housewives also know that a package comes in from the store every once in a while with weevils, moth worms, or worse. The frame in the bedroom contained split peas, corn seeds, and red beans in its various compartments; three different kinds of bugs had been dining for some time. It was immediately banished from the house, and its contents were dumped at the bird feeder. The empty frame itself was left outside in case it had eggs in it.

If you share my Yankee aversion to wasting things, you'll understand that it bothered me to see that frame out there doing nothing. I couldn't bear to throw it away, so finally I took it apart, scrubbed it well, baked the wooden parts several hours in a slow oven, and treated the plastic windows to several doses of bleach and hot water.

I remember that a friend had confided how she had filled one of these frames with interesting bits of the natural world. This is a really great idea; instead of static, insect-attracting seeds, make it into a small display case for some favorite things. (I gave mine a shot of insecticide before I sealed the frame. You might also hide a mothball somewhere.)

Special pine cones, an empty wasp nest on a twig (make sure there are no babies in the combs), an old praying mantis egg case from which all the hatchlings have long gone, the discarded chrysalis of a cicada, a beautiful lichen, shells, mineral specimens, or just appealing stones are all possibilities for a small section. A tall compartment might take some pussy willows, a twig with acorns still attached, a piece of dried vine with seeds or berries too fragile to display without protection, or a few long pods from wisteria or honey locust.

The birds where I live are prone to leave whole eggs on the ground. It is against the law to collect bird nests, but you can make a small one yourself from excelsior or straw to hold an egg so found or even the empty halves of one that managed to hatch. If you have a lovely dried flower, glue a butterfly to it. My broccoli bed attracts many small white cabbage butterflies, but if the frame is large enough, you could use one compartment for a bigger species. This is a perfect place for such fragile beauties as the dried seed heads of wild asters or summer phlox.

My resourceful friend also suggested covering the back of the frame with a piece of pretty cloth. She used light blue velvet, which set off the contents so perfectly that I followed suit, putting it in place before I glued the back window back in. The extra edges of the cloth were trimmed off after the glue dried.

Bookends
Materials:

 pair of plain metal student bookends
 self-stick burlap
 white glue
 assorted dried materials, seashells, or minerals
 felt (optional)
 edging (optional)
 clear glaze spray

I don't know which chapter to put these in, but the techniques are very similar to those for the hangings, so I'm appending them here. They are incredibly easy to make, but quite lovely and different-looking.

You could probably use almost any kind of material to cover the metal, but the self-stick burlap is ideal in whatever plain color you prefer. Self-sticking vinyl shelf covering in a plain color is another possibility. Make all measurements and cut your pieces before you remove the backing. As you can see in Fig. 7-9, I also covered the hole in the front of the bookend with this background material.

First lay the material inside the right angle of the outside of the bookend. With a pencil mark a line on the paper backing about ½ in. bigger on all sides and cut out the first piece. Peel back about an inch of the backing and place the top of the bookend on the sticky side so that the ½ in. margin shows at both top and sides. Now peel off the rest of the backing and smooth the piece downwards into the right angle, then all the way to the other end. Make sure there are no bubbles or wrinkles by smoothing as you go. With scissors make two slash cuts at the front corners of the bottom, one at each side of the right angle, and two more at each point on the top where the curve begins. This mitering allows you to bend the overlapping margins around to stick on the back without an unsightly bulge at the corner and the angle.

Now cut a T-shaped piece of felt or self-stick material for the bottom where the bookend will sit. Measure it to fit exactly the shape of the metal at the front and back. You will get a more durable surface if you cut the felt on the two wings of the T a little larger than the metal on the back edge; make a cut in the felt at the corner so you can bend the extra felt back against the upright. Glue on so it covers the overlap from the

front piece and extends to the curved end of the metal that goes under the books. This piece not only protects the overlaps on the bottom from any wear but also guards against scratching your furniture.

The last step is to cut a piece of the self-stick material as close as you can to the exact size of the upright back of the bookend. Peel off the backing, and fit the material on so that it perfectly hides the overlaps from the front and the two felt overlaps but has nothing extending over to show on the outside.

Only very durable materials should be used to decorate the outside of the bookend, because it will be subjected to a certain amount of pushing. I glued the green magnolia leaf, some sea-oat sheaves, and a yellow strawflower against the back, but I hoped that no one would put any pressure there. The long white pine cones on either side and the round cone and sweet-gum balls at the bottom are very strong and should be able to take a great deal of punishment.

Use plenty of glue when attaching the ornaments to the bookends so they will not work loose. I did the round cone and the sweet-gums first, let them dry well, and then glued the leaf, oats, and white pine cones in another sitting. I propped the bookends with that surface flat to dry for a whole day before going on to put in the finishing touches of the strawflower, acorn, and beech burr.

The entire front surface of the bookend was given three good coats of clear glaze spray on three different days to provide a strong, protective finish.

Since they are very strong, seashells are naturals for an item like this. So are mineral specimens. If you have something very durable at the center front where the hand is most likely to exert pressure on the bookend, you can fill in the back with slightly finer things, but I would avoid anything very fragile. I'm not too sure about those magnolia leaves, although they are nearly flat against the background and somewhat out of the way. The three coats of glaze gave them added strength.

Whatever you decide to use, take time to lay it out tentatively before you start gluing. The friend who gave me the idea glued braid on the entire outer edge of the front of the bookend before decorating it. This step is entirely optional.

8
min–
iatures
of many
kinds

Fig. 8-1. Pussy willow bunnies at play in a miniature shadow box. The swing actually moves, but the seesaw is glued in place. Trees are small branches of pearly everlasting. Rabbit ears are wings of pine seeds.

Fig. 8-2. Rabbits on a flat base decorated with a dogwood twig tree, moss, strawflowers, and a small rock, all glued in place. The bird in the tree is made with an immature pine cone, and the nest is an acorn cup with bayberry eggs.

Anyone who has ever loved a dollhouse empathizes with the world of miniatures. To judge by the ads in some magazines, miniatures have become a great field for adult collectors who pay enormous sums for exact replicas of elaborate furniture and antiques. The trouble with the boughten miniature is that it is often too expensive to do anything with except lock away in a display case. And that takes away all the fun. So here are some miniatures you can make from the bounties of nature for your children to play with, to brighten up an invalid's room, or for that someone who has everything.

The trick is to make a tiny scene or situation. It can take place in an enclosed shadow box or on a flat base. The latter I find a bit easier to make because the open space allows more latitude than the confining box. I've made some suggestions for situations, accessories, and little people and animals that you can put in the scenes, but I hope these will be only jumping-off points for your own imagination.

Favorite hobbies, sports, or places of the recipient are one inspiration, and neither age nor sex seems to make much difference. My teenager was just as delighted with her scene showing the champion Philadelphia Flyers on the ice as her grandmother was with an old-fashioned corn-husk doll skipping rope. A three-year-old can conjure up all sorts of magic just by looking into the little Christmas room in Fig. C-25. My scene of Washington crossing the Delaware drew pleased comments from any number of sophisticated adults.

Used with restraint, a few props can make your scene more graphic. In the Christmas box I fashioned a fireplace from a scrap of Styrofoam, glued some felt stockings to it, added a rug made from a scrap of wool material, and wrapped some tiny packages to glue in place under the tree.

Usually, however, I try to make the accessories from natural materials. For one thing, this is a challenge; for another, it means that your scene is absolutely unique. This is something to remember when making a miniature for the someone who has everything. Somewhere in the world there is a copy of the most expensive Dresden figurine, but yours are guaranteed one-of-a-kinds.

Bases

Woodworking shops and hobby centers often carry shadow boxes. You don't want the fancy mitered sort that is hung up like a picture, but rather one that will sit on a surface. The deeper it is, the better. My Christmas box is nearly 3 in. deep and was much easier to work with than the bunny on the swing, which is hardly 1¾ in. deep. If you wish, you can cover one or both open sides with clear plastic wrap after the scene is complete. Or you can make a solid backdrop for one side.

Other scenes are set up on bases. My favorites are very thin slices of a big log, which can either be bought in craft centers or homemade if you have access to a chain saw and the skill to use it. Woodcutters offer all sorts of finished bases, but I prefer the rustic effect of a rougher log for this kind of work. George Washington's adventure is set up on a thin slab of beech picked out of fireplace wood from the sawmill. It is even possible to make a tiny scene to insert in a large glass container or on a base to be covered with a large Victorian glass dome.

Accessories

Your own ingenuity will add many items to this list, but here are some of the most useful to give life to

Fig. 8-3. Thistles and milkweed silk form the hair of pixies warming themselves by a log fire. Foliage on the tree is green-dyed reindeer lichen glued in place.

your scenes (I keep a box of these around and add to it as opportunity arises):

dried moss and small sprigs of dried grass
small hemlock and spruce cones
tiny immature acorns
very small leaves, dried or pressed
twiggy tree branches to make trees
shrub twigs with tiny branches to make trees
dried goldenrod for trees and shrubs (spray green if desired)
shrub or tree branches for stumps and logs
very small assorted strawflowers
interesting small stones
broken mirrors for ice
broken glass for water
small, very full juniper branches (dyed with soft green floral spray, these make evergreen trees and bushes)
bayberries for birds' eggs
acorn cups for birds' nests
very small seashells
lichens of all sorts
tiny, dried mushrooms
dyed reindeer lichen (green)
green hobby grass (sold for model train setups)
sandpaper for beach or playground
odd pieces of balsa wood
empty nut shells
scraps of Styrofoam
floral clay

Situations

Depending on the sport or activity involved, your scene will take place in a particular season. This suggests certain props to set the mood.

In winter you might have a scene showing skating, sledding, tobogganing, or skiing. Snow made from a thick glop of soap flakes and a few drops of water is obviously an appropriate filler. You can even make a snowman or an igloo out of this mixture. The trees will be bare, and no flowers will be showing, but moss, dried grass, stumps, logs, and a few dried leaves help to set the tone. Stumps and logs can be glued directly to the base, but trees need more support. I stick the tree in a glob of floral clay or a piece of

Styrofoam, and glue that to the base. The raw base can then be hidden by gluing some moss around it. Use the same treatment to hide the edges of the pond. A few small logs cut with pruning shears can be piled log cabin fashion to suggest a fire. I have some orange-dyed grass that looks just like flames.

Balsa is easy to carve for skis and sleds, and a wood shaving from a plane creates a great toboggan. I made hockey sticks for my Flyers from twigs with cantaloupe seeds glued to the ends and a puck from a very small wisteria seed stuck to the mirror.

For any season, you can suggest a cave by gluing some small rocks together and packing moss between them. A short section of a large branch with a hole carved in it by nature makes a great tree house; you can even make a door for it from a piece of balsa.

Summertime activities include fishing, gardening, jumping rope, picnics, and playgrounds. A piece of ordinary glass with some blue foil glued to its underside recreates water, and any stick and a piece of string becomes a fishing pole. A picnic table is simple with two X's of thin wood and a piece of balsa for the top. My swing is nothing more than a small piece of wood for the seat and very thin wire (gauge 28) for the supports. It actually swings. The seesaw is a flat piece of wood glued to a small log. A piece of twine

Fig. 8-4. See the text for a description of the hats
in this fashion show.

can be stiffened with starch, sugar water, or white
glue so that it will stay in the air when fastened to a
figure jumping rope. Walnut-shell halves make cra-
dles; or with a few bits of balsa and some acorn cups
for wheels, you can turn them into wagons, baby
carriages, or wheelbarrows. One of my daughters
built a miniature jungle gym from pieces of toothpicks!

A summer garden scene is easy to suggest with
paths, rocks, grass, and dried flowers. If you don't
like goldenrod trees, try gluing a few pieces of green
reindeer lichen to a twig. The same treatment on a
small branch of pearly everlasting produces a flowering tree more easily than fastening tiny starflowers to
a twig.

One clever friend created a band concert with a
huge dried mushroom for the shell. Her musicians
played horns made of cut-down golf tees, clanged
cymbals which were really two small sand dollars,
and strummed a banjo made from an acorn cup and a
toothpick. The leader, of course, held a baton.

Another friend took *The Owl and the Pussycat* as
her theme and made a pea-green boat from a carefully cleaned empty avocado shell. The only limit
here is ingenuity to match your imagination.

Dramatis Personae
No matter how great the scenery, your miniature
needs some characters to tell a good story. They can
either be animals or little people. The latter are
much easier to make, but some situations call for
animals. Remember that the figures must be small
to stay in scale with the scene.

Whether you call them pixies, elves, or lep-
rechauns, the little people are at least as much fun to
make as to play with. Depending on the situation in
which you put them and the materials you use for
their manufacture, you can depict almost any character. Hats are a great way to establish their character.
Take those in Fig. 8-4. Reading from left to right: the
little guy in the beech-burr chapeau can fit into any
long-hair situation; the one with the spent Canadian
thistle cap is made-to-order for winter sports; the
swami's hat is two-thirds of a green Japanese lantern;
the pirate has a swashbuckling number made from a
dried datura calyx and a cut-down bird feather; a
hollowed-out spruce-cone tip tops the guru, who
could also double as Robin Hood or a Himalayan
guide; the admiral wears a sliver of horse-chestnut
burr and a chicken feather; lastly, the acorn-cup
beanie goes everywhere. End of fashion show.

123

Fig. 8-5. Ruffles of this large larch cone make it ideal for a girl pixie's body.

Going even farther afield ("addled" is my husband's description), I cut small circles of felt, bent them to look like tricornes, glued them in place, and sewed cockades of red, white, and blue yarn for the Revolutionary patriots crossing the Delaware in Fig. C-21. Milkweed silk previously glued to their acorn heads made wigs. The ordinary soldier's was merely trimmed with sharp scissors, but George's was tied together with a piece of thread to form a peruke.

Scraps of material and lace can be used to make all kinds of hats from sunbonnets to turbans. I had to make sure that my hockey players were identified as champion Flyers rather than just any old team, so I made a scarf for each by braiding strands of orange, black, and white wool, since Philadelphia's favorites wear those colors. Goodness only knows where all of this can lead.

Hair helps too. In addition to the wonderfully useful milkweed silk, yarn can be braided or glued into almost any kind of hairdo. Spent Canadian thistles often have a few strands of silk, and they make great old men, with or without their caps. The leader in the aforementioned band concert sported hair made from a dried clematis pod, and he looked as wild as any musician could ever be.

Bodies are the easiest of all. The best are made from small Scotch pine cones that have not quite opened fully. Press them down a little to flatten the bottom so they will stand well when you glue them in place. Their shape is such that they need no arms to look quite alive. Douglas fir cones that have odd bracts sticking out are also a possibility (see the swami). Casuarina cones make very small bodies. Larch cones are slightly frilled and look like a full skirt.

All my characters' heads are made from acorns glued so that the tips become the pixies' noses. While making these little people or the animals described next, have a supply of tacky, vintage white glue around so you don't have to do too much propping while it dries. You can also put a bit of glue on both parts and allow them almost to dry before pressing together. Tweezers are a handy tool for this work. Acrylic paint in a tube is perfect for eyes, eyebrows, and mouths. I don't even use a brush; I just take a little paint directly from the tube with a toothpick.

You'd rather use tiny animals to provide the action in your scene? With all of the zoological world at your fingertips, there's no telling what you can come up with, but here are some of my favorites:

Mouse: body—large acorn; head—small acorn; ears—two very small empty acorn cups; whiskers—milkweed silk; tail—brown string. Paint on eyes.

Rabbit: body—large pussy willow; tail—tiny pill of cotton; head—small pussy willow; long ears—wings from two pine seeds (shake any ripe pine cone, and some will fall out, but cut off the seed before gluing); nose and eyes—small black seeds or tiny beads. Both rabbits and the cats described below can either sit or stand, depending on how you place the head on the body.

Cat: body—large pussy willow: tail—small fluffy chicken feather; head—small pussy willow; short, pointed ears—triangles cut from either pine seed wings or a handy pod; nose and eyes—small black seeds or tiny beads.

Owl: body—very small, immature Scotch or Austrian pine cone; head—even smaller, similar cone (the body cone is used vertically, and the head cone is glued horizontally to its fat top, as in Fig. C-22); ears and beak—triangles cut from any kind of pod; eyes—single flowers of pearly everlasting, starflowers, or single seeds from an althea pod.

Larger animals such as the turkeys and the owls in Figs. C-8 and C-10 are even easier to fashion, because there is a wider variety of big cones and pods. Use the same techniques as with miniatures. Such figures may be mounted on bases or used with greens or other suitable accessories if desired.

Dollhouse Decorations

No little girl wants her dollhouse to remain undecorated for the holidays. You can give her a wreath by making a ring of wire 2–3 in. in diameter. (I once used a broken hoop earring.) Using the continuous wiring method and very thin wire, fasten tiny sprigs of fine-needled juniper around the frame. Coat when done with green floral spray, and it will stay good for years. Glue on a proportional red bow and tiny beads or small pods for decoration. A dollhouse Christmas tree is constructed in the same way with a straight piece of juniper. The tree in my box is glued into a stand made from the gold top of a perfume bottle, which was filled with floral clay to weight it down.

When I was young, I made candlesticks for my dollhouse out of spent 22 rifle shells and birthday candles. You can form even prettier ones by gluing a small, empty acorn cup to a larger one. The lower cup should be round side up, and the top one reversed so the birthday candle can be glued inside it.

The same basic candlestick can be used to make a menorah. After the glue between the two acorn cups is dry, glue on a long slender piece of twig or part of a milkweed pod, centering it on the acorn cup. Then glue tiny stubs of birthday candles on the top of the holder.

Using the thinnest willow wands, balsa wood, odd cones and pods, and small dried flowers, you can make all sorts of furniture and decorations for a dollhouse. Years from now the daughter for whom you made them will remember your efforts far more clearly than the most expensive, elaborate miniature that you could possibly buy her. Working together on such a project, you'll foster a closeness that will do a lot for your future relationship.

Unfortunately, boys are not encouraged to play with dollhouses, which I think is very sad. A girl gets rid of frustrations and learns to give her imagination free rein through such an outlet. You can achieve almost the same effect for a boy without having to worry about what you're doing to his psyche by giving him a zoo, farm, or simple model train scene. These need little dolls to people them and will also accommodate all sorts of strange animals. Teach your children of both sexes how to use a jackknife safely, and start them out with a few suggestions so that they too can have the fun of directing a miniature world.

Miniature Arrangements

Shy people who would not dream of entering a fancy flower show or even of trying an elaborate design on their own families don't seem to have the same inhibitions about miniature arrangements. With dried flowers, grasses, and pods, you don't have to worry about water to keep anything alive, so you can use the smallest sort of container, even one which cannot hold any water at all.

Tiny baskets, bottle tops, or lipstick caps, among other things, can be utilized for containers, but the natural world has some good offerings too. You can glue a big pod such as a yucca to a small piece of bark and fill it carefully with a few sprigs of statice and some starflowers. The boat-shaped milkweed pod glued to a base makes another fine container for a simple bouquet or an arrangement of miniature pods and cones.

Seashells are perfect too, especially small conchs and snails. The spineless sea urchin found at low tide on rocky northern coasts can be pried loose and left in the sun until its insides dry out. Glued to a sand-dollar base, it makes a lovely vase for a diminutive bouquet, and the delicate branches of sea lavender, which grows on the tidal flats of the East Coast, are very much in keeping to fill it. So are sea oats and almost any grass or small dried flower. Again, these are starting points. Do some beachcombing, and see where your imagination flies.

Any of these miniature arrangements can be used as is, or they can be popped into a glass container, as described in Chapter 9. Either way they are perfect for party or shower favors or a sickroom decoration. (They do not encourage the bacteria now suspected in fresh flower containers.) They are just as good for a hostess gift or simply to enjoy yourself.

9
dried beauty under glass

Some people just aren't gardeners. They either cannot or will not get out there to dig and weed. Give them the healthiest house plant, and in no time it falters. Yet many of these same friends love the color of flowers and appreciate the form and patterns of the natural world.

Dried beauty under glass is just the ticket for them. Properly done, these bouquets last many years; the only requirement is to dust or wash the outside of the glass container from time to time. I have some more than five years old that are as fresh-looking as on the day they were made.

With enough patience, I suppose you could even fashion one in a thin-necked bottle, but the material you use is very brittle, so I wouldn't suggest that for the novice. What you want is a clear-glass container with a top. You could use one of colored glass, since the plants inside do not need sunlight for growing, but the effect of tinted glass spoils the interplay of colors in most arrangements.

For something temporary, you can even utilize a container without a cover, such as a big brandy snifter. After a few months, however, it will grow very dusty, and even the backflow of the vacuum cleaner will not clean it well. Any terrarium suggested for living plants is a possibility, as are the clear plastic square and rectangular boxes in gift shops. The Victorian glass dome on a base is perfect for a dried arrangement and is regaining popularity.

Many glass factories have a selection of apothecary jars in all shapes and sizes. I prefer round ones to squares; squatty shapes rather limit the material you can use, because of the lack of height. One very graceful type is shaped like a pear. Brandy snifters are hard to get tops for, but sometimes you can utilize an old watch crystal or a laboratory culture dish as a cap. Glue it in place, or it will surely flip off and break during a dusting.

If you have access to a glass cutter and enough skill, you can use almost any kind of jar by trimming off its ugly screw rings and fitting on your own clear top from a blank of glass or clear, hard plastic. I do not recommend the jars with cork lids often available in gift shops, because part of the effect is lost if you cannot look through from the top. Theoretically, you could glue on a top of clear plastic wrap, but in practice this is hard to do.

If all else fails, buy a small globe at the dime store. Provide some kind of base to which you will attach the arrangement, then invert the bowl over it, and glue to the base. The flat bottom of this detracts a bit when viewed from above, and it is not easy to get the small neck of the globe over the arrangement, but it can be done.

Whatever container you choose, make sure that it is perfectly clean and dry. All material to be used must be absolutely dry too, otherwise you will find that mold appears and spoils the sealed world you have created.

Use Oasis (available at all florist shops) rather than Styrofoam for the base. It is much softer, so you can stick the brittle stems of the dried items into it without breakage. Oasis is easily cut into any shape with a sharp knife. The base should be at least 2 in. smaller than the diameter of the jar. If the arrangement is done properly, none of the base will show when you have finished. Rather than wasting Oasis to make round bases, I usually cut a square or rectangle and bevel its four corners slightly to obtain a roundish mound.

Except for the very largest containers, you will be working with rather small items. I find tweezers an absolute must for placing much of the material in the Oasis. Many of the items will also have hard, brittle stems, which are more wisely cut with wire cutters than with your good scissors. Some bought materials, such as big strawflowers, even have wire stems.

If you have to purchase much material, you will be appalled at the prices. Having a garden helps, as does a sharp eye whem roaming fields and roadsides. From my own garden I harvest pearly everlasting, butterfly-weed, perennial statice and baby's breath, pussy willows, artemisia, tansy, small clematis pods, armeria, alliums, globe amaranths, brixa and other grasses, yarrow, heather, and celosia. You can grow some of the larger strawflowers too. From the wild I gather bittersweet, sea lavender, Queen-Anne's-lace (which I often dye pink and blue), golden alexander, goldenrod, mountain mint, spent wild asters, and a wide assortment of pods, cones, and seed capsules.

Fig. 9-2. Cattail and large wisteria pod give height to this dried arrangement for a large brandy snifter. Grasses were picked while green in the author's garden and dried upside down. The container should be kept nearby when making these conceits so the arrangement will fit the space available.

Preparation of all of these is detailed in Chapter 1.

If you are an expert in drying flowers, you will have a whole storehouse of material at hand, from dried rosebuds to bright zinnias. Most of us are not so dedicated. No matter how provident you are, you will still have to buy some dried materials, but if you store them dust-free, they stay good indefinitely. Over the years you can accumulate a varied supply.

Dyed immortelles and certain grasses can be a good investment. You cannot make dried terrariums without some of the tiny dyed starflowers, and the small floral butts and hillflowers are also very useful. These three are dyed in a wide variety of colors. They are usually imported and are not cheap, but you get them by the bunch. Start with a few colors that appeal to you. The batches vary widely due to the dyes. Most blues are muddy, but if you find a bright, true blue, snatch it quickly; this is the hardest color to find in dried material, even though it is one of the handiest. Every shopping mall and many gift shops have bunches of starflowers at least part of the year, so you should have no trouble finding them.

Also handy as fillers to hide the base are green-dyed reindeer moss (it is naturally a soft gray color, but this is hard to find), chartreuse lichen from the West Coast, green-dyed lycopodium (it looks like tiny evergreen trees), and dried moss (which you can buy in small assorted packages).

What you do about pretty stones or even fake accessories, which range from elves to mushrooms, is up to you. Personally, I think most of them are awful. Dried lichens like British soldiers can be worked into some arrangements, and they are much softer than the blatant copies. I often perch a small butterfly caught in my garden on top of a flower in my dry terrariums.

Let's suppose that you have no training at all in flower arrangement. A couple of rules will take you a long way. Generally, the larger the flower, the closer to the base it should go. Keep in mind how things grow naturally, and don't poke just one straight stalk upright; rather face things down, and try to slant them a bit. You can't bend the stiff fine stems of the starflowers, for example, but you can put a group of them together, varying the heights and having all the stems rise from the same general area in a fountain effect. If the stems of the first things that you put in place are very stiff-looking, remember that you can hide them later with some filler material. Some variation in shape and color among your materials makes for interest, but try to repeat some of the things to guard against a too spotty effect. Choose colors which harmonize. Generally, it is more aesthetically pleasing to have an odd number of the same flower in a group.

Above all, strive to make the tiny arrangement you are fashioning as tall and as wide as the container in which it will reside. I always keep the container beside me on the table where I work so I can measure from time to time. Items like artemisia, pearly everlasting, and perennial statice have a little elasticity even when dry, so I use those for establishing the limits of height and breadth; they will give a bit when I put the completed arrangement in the container. They also tend to dry with a bit of a curve, which is more graceful for the edges.

One last reminder: the container arrangement is apt to be viewed from more than one side. Fashion it so that it can be enjoyed from whatever angle it is seen. You are working in the round, in other words.

How to Make a Dried Terrarium

Materials:

    covered clear glass container
    white glue and dip pot
    Oasis
    assorted dried flowers
    dried moss, lichens, grasses, etc.

Having assembled your ingredients, first choose what you will use for the bigger flowers. Even in a small container I try to use at least two of these so there is a focal point on either side of the jar. If you use large, yellow strawflowers, you may wish to add red or orange starflowers and a few tiny groups of contrasting blue. The perennial statice dries white, and the pearly everlasting is a soft cream; I always have a large supply of them on hand to blend in with everything. The statice has such graceful lines, and the stemless flowers of the pearly everlasting can be painstakingly glued on at the end to hide the base, so I recommend both of these highly. I'll use my favorite materials and the apothecary jar pictured in Fig. 9-3, which is 5–6 in. tall and about 3 in. in diameter, as an example of how to do the job.

Put the item that is to establish the ultimate height of the arrangement in place first by measuring it against the container. Then dip its stem in the glue, and stick into the center of the Oasis. I like a piece of perennial statice for this. Now cut the stems of the two big dried flowers in proportion to the ultimate width and height of the arrangement; I usually have one so short that it almost rests on the Oasis, the other 1–2 in. longer. Dip their ends in the glue, and stick into the Oasis. Now work gradually smaller pieces of statice around the center to make a miniature bush, which serves to hide the wire stem of the taller strawflower. Have some of the statice extend out as far as the size of the container will allow on all sides of the base.

Fill in with some moss or lichen for a greenish note here and there and to hide the base. By now you'll be using the tweezers and holding the base up in one hand to do your gluing. Cut some short-stemmed starflowers, dip each stem in glue with the tweezers, then force gently into the Oasis. The reindeer lichen and the moss are both soft and fluffy, so you can "plant" a patch of the starflowers right through them. Add a small grouping of tiny clematis balls on one side, then put a group of contrasting starflowers on the other. Now glue almost stemless bunches of the pearly everlasting with the tweezers wherever the base still shows. The irregularity of the everlasting sticking out beyond the base helps to make the arrangement look more natural. Keep turning the base so that it looks finished from all angles.

One caution: the white glue dries hard. It is better to complete the whole arrangement in one sitting or at least to do all the finishing touches to hide the base at one time. Otherwise you may be unable to push the brittle starflower stems through the dried glue. Try not to smear any extra glue around, even though it does dry clear.

Once satisfied with the arrangement, allow it to dry for an hour or so to make sure that everything will stay as you want it. Then drop a few globs of glue onto the center of the bottom of the container. Using all your ingenuity, tilt the arrangement to one side slightly to get it into the container without disturbing the glued material. Slide it down, and press it into the small pool of glue so that it stands upright.

Replace the lid, and you're done, unless you wish to tie a dainty ribbon around the knob on the top. If you must take or send this arrangement anywhere, stick the top down firmly with a bit of masking tape to keep it safe. I have sent arrangements successfully through the mail by sitting them in large, heavy cardboard boxes with lots of crumpled newspaper on all four sides of the glass containers so they cannot move or be crushed.

Variation: particularly for St. Valentine's Day, you can fashion a slightly different kind of bouquet for a favorite someone. Using a small, round paper doily, cut out a section like a piece of pie along the radius of the circle, and push the doily together until you have a small cone. Glue it together. When dry, fold the outer edges of the doily downward over the V of the cone. Glue a small piece of Oasis in the cone, and put one big strawflower in the very center. Now, with small starflowers and other diminutive items make concentric circles around the center. A few small sprigs of statice or baby's breath extending over the

Figs. 9-3 and 9-4. No matter what the shape of the container, the arrangement inside should try to fill as much space as possible.

130

cone give it a dainty air. You can paste a red heart or a tiny red bow on the white collar of the cone if you like. Again, put a daub of glue on the bottom of the container, and force your nosegay down until it is resting against the glue so that it cannot move around. This conceit is especially pretty in a low, squat container.

Variation: with a very large container like a Victorian dome or a brandy snifter, you have greater latitude in what you can use for the focal points and for the high item in the center. Try cattails, long twisted wisteria pods, pampas plumes, pussy willows, or a bunch of dangly grass-like sea oats or brixa for the latter. Dried thistles, cardoon puffs, small pine cones, deodara roses, or wood roses make interesting focal points. You will still fill in with some smaller materials and hide the base with foundation items like moss and lichen, but the whole effect will be bolder. With some of these bigger dried things, the overall color scheme is likely to be in browns and creams with touches of color, which makes an ideal arrangement for a man.

Figs. 9-5 and 9-6. Paper doily forms the edging for a nosegay to be put under glass. Oasis glued in the center of the cone makes a firm base on which to glue dried flowers.

Index